The Garden at LEVENS

The Garden at
LEVENS

CHRIS CROWDER

Photographs by Vivian Russell

FRANCES LINCOLN

For Lydia, Emily and
Nicholas

Frances Lincoln Limited
4 Torriano Mews, Torriano Avenue
London NW5 2RZ
www.franceslincoln.com

The Garden at Levens
Copyright © Frances Lincoln Limited 2005
Text copyright © Chris Crowder 2005
Photographs copyright © Vivian Russell 2005
(with the exception of those listed on page
160)
Plan of the garden on pages 6–7
copyright © Jean Sturgis 2005

First Frances Lincoln edition 2005

A catalogue record for this book is
available from the British Library.

Printed and bound in China

ISBN 0 7112 2434 X

9 8 7 6 5 4 3 2 1

PAGES 2–3 Black tulips
beneath Beaumont's House,
against the background of the
Topiary Garden
RIGHT Linking the garden
with the landscape: looking
across the ha-ha to the field
and avenue

Contents

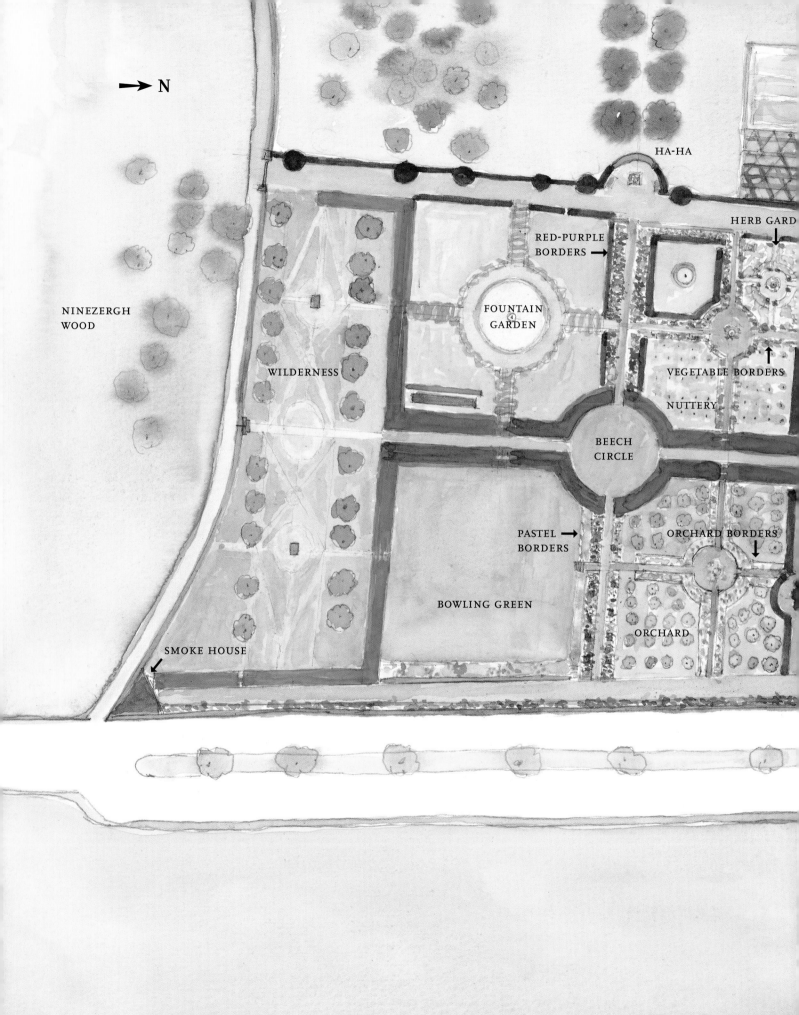

N

NINEZERGH
WOOD

HA-HA

RED-PURPLE
BORDERS

HERB GARD

FOUNTAIN
GARDEN

WILDERNESS

VEGETABLE BORDERS

NUTTERY

BEECH
CIRCLE

PASTEL
BORDERS

ORCHARD BORDERS

BOWLING GREEN

ORCHARD

SMOKE HOUSE

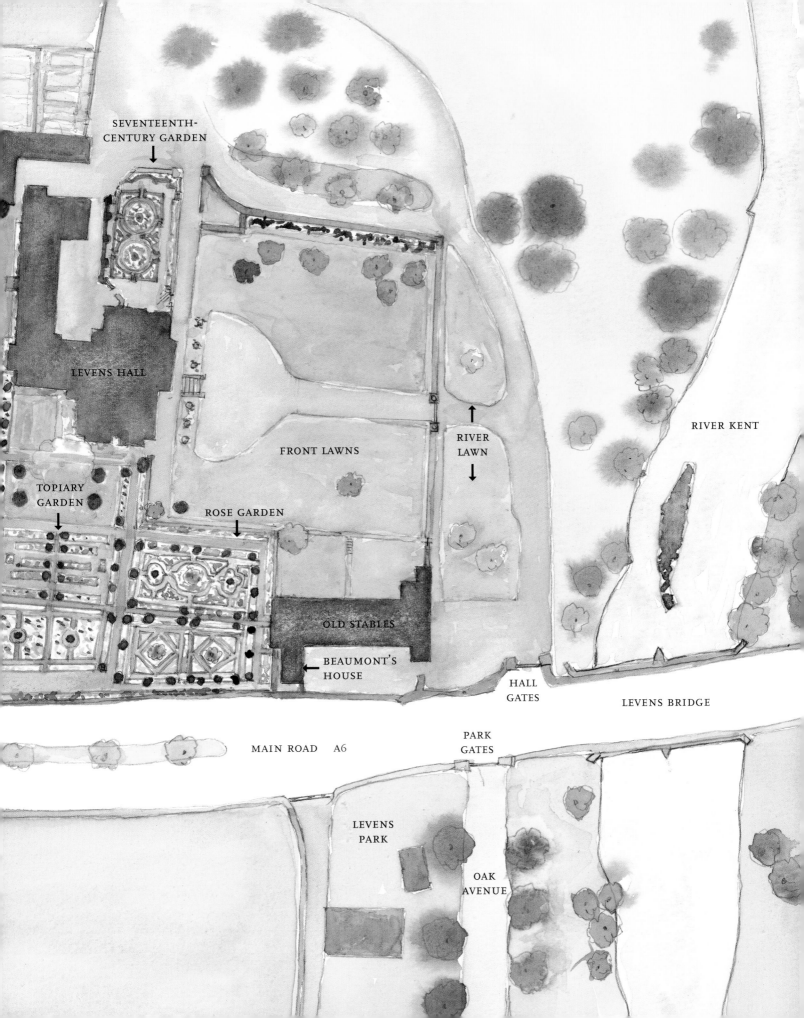

SEVENTEENTH-
CENTURY GARDEN

LEVENS HALL

TOPIARY
GARDEN

ROSE GARDEN

FRONT LAWNS

RIVER
LAWN

RIVER KENT

OLD STABLES

BEAUMONT'S
HOUSE

HALL
GATES

LEVENS BRIDGE

MAIN ROAD   A6

PARK
GATES

LEVENS PARK

OAK
AVENUE

INTRODUCTION

Twenty years have passed since I first wandered awestruck and amazed beneath Levens' ancient topiary.

A fantastical gathering of giant green overblown mushrooms, leaning loaves, tall, teetering towers and ballooning bulbous blimps of yew, with smaller, almost human forms and figures in rounded box beneath them, have been caught, freeze-framed, in an absurd dance, their contorted movement stilled in some surreal Disney or Daliesque scene. By day this assemblage of tipsy, jovial, party characters jostle for attention, bringing a smile to even the most serious and sober of guests. By night an altogether eerier drama unfolds. As dusk falls and a cool dampness pervades the air, the garden becomes the old yews' own world once more as a quiet solitude, even melancholy, descends. Their looming dark outlines are silhouetted against the night sky as deep, inky-black shadows creep across moonlit lawns. They infuse the stillness with an unsettling, otherworldly presence. Watching . . . waiting . . .

As the new, young head gardener I saw and felt all this, and I was also deeply moved by the sense of great antiquity and continuity expressed in these ancient forms, which are living testament to centuries of skilled, patient care and hand craftsmanship. Unnamed gardeners for ten generations and more worked this soil and worked out their lives amongst these venerable trees. Now it was for me to take my place in that lineage. To these old garden aristocrats, our human span must seem to fly by like the passing seasons. Within a mere three score years and ten we germinate, grow, prosper and return to dust. Like leaves that unfold, live for a summer then wither, fall and blow away, we are ephemeral and transitory. We who work there share for a short time only a space that is the trees', not ours.

The topiary does not represent anything in particular as individual pieces, other than what we imagine; as a collective group, however, it has become the image that defines the garden, a landscape of great visual public statement that evokes within us all very personal feelings. Resonating with echoes from a past age, surviving largely as it was created at the end of the seventeenth century, it is a garden full of its own memories, but it also shares with us so much more than this old, green, dream-like fantasy.

Beyond the massive clipped hedge walls of the Topiary Garden, the gardens lie quartered and quartered again. Leafy divisions separate a series of secluded and secret chambers linked through intriguing passageways and openings, and constantly enticing you on with snatched glimpses of new vistas. Here there is movement from light to shade, from fullness of form to space and void, from intensity of effect to restful pools of contemplative peace. The garden is indeed greater than the topiary alone.

Aerial view of Levens Hall and garden

The topiary in early
spring: ancient forms
remade, sharpened and
redefined for the season
ahead

Three centuries have gone by since this small corner of Westmorland was enclosed and the seeds of all this were sown. The dead hand of history does not lie heavily on these old bones, though. Garden fashions have come, gone, and often come round again during those years, but although the Levens landscape has never been totally destroyed to make way for the new, neither has it atrophied: it has always been influenced subtly by the cultural and artistic expression of the time. The garden wears its heritage lightly, shaped but not bound by it, conveying still a sense of growth, vibrancy and development. It somehow remains forward looking, living for today and tomorrow, not just in the past. This is no preserved relic, or recent restoration, but a living, growing vision, recreated, and truly remade afresh each year.

I would describe the greatest influence on my approach to this garden as not horticultural writers, strangely enough, but that great eighteenth-century freethinker and radical Thomas Paine. Through his common-sense writings on religion and the rights of man, he ushered in a new age of reason. Speaking directly to his audience in a language that cut clearly through to their hearts, he fired revolutions in America, France and very nearly England too. His work helped change the world, and it reads as powerfully and truthfully now as then. Although his thoughts on gardening are not recorded, one of the central themes of his philosophy was that no generation should be chained to the past or could imprison the future. This is as valid a notion in the garden as in government.

Simplicity and repetition are key themes: here the bold purple of cannas gives way to a vegetable garden vista lined by pole bean wigwams and courgettes

His influence manifests itself in my work at Levens in that I endeavour to maintain the garden's openness to contemporary cultural influences. Although the garden is ancient, I – and those who work with me – garden it for our time and our eyes, effectively breathing new life into it. The way people see and interpret a landscape changes slowly but constantly, and we now see life through the selective framing, focus and filter of the camera lens. We are the sound-bite generation, and our view of the world is told as a story for us passive recipients through magazines, newspapers and television. The garden at Levens therefore works and is worked as a series of distinct photo opportunities; it is presented as a series of visual hits for maximum sensual impact and effect. Key elements are distilled, repeated and emphasized, and distractions and dilutants removed. No special language or education is required to understand it; the meaning is clearly conveyed to all.

In this book, the story of the garden at Levens, I attempt to unfold the pages of a living history, and to tell the tale of our own time. This story will continue, though, and my part within it is just a chapter in the whole, part of a journey, not the destination, informing but not governing what will follow; the twenty years that have passed since I first came to Levens is not long in this old garden's eyes. I hope I succeed in sharing here a little of the interest and great pleasure it has given me as I play my small part in shaping history.

HISTORICAL BACKGROUND

THE EARLY YEARS

The garden at Levens is rightly famous throughout the world, not just for what it is now but also for its great age and the fact that the fascinating accounts of those who helped shape it so many centuries ago still exist and can breathe life into its long history. They link us with the past, and give us an appreciation of our part in the future.

The garden occupies an area of low-lying land on the banks of the River Kent. The Lakeland fells rise in the distance to the north and the great limestone massif of Whitbarrow dominates views to the west; its southern extremity abruptly terminates in the dramatic cliffs of White Scar overlooking the Kent estuary and the vast tidal expanse of Morecambe Bay. Marsh, forest and wild hill scenery would have defined the landscape before drainage, felling and agriculture took hold.

Although little is known of the garden before the 1690s, there had been a building at Levens for many centuries before then. The earliest ownership records can be traced back to 1170 when a charter from William de Lancaster granted land at Levens to Norman de Hieland, while reserving for himself the rights to fishing, hawking and hunting. This Norman later assumed the name de Redman, from which the nearby village of Yealand Redmayne derives its name, and his family went on to hold Levens for the next 400 years.

It is not known whether there was a building on this site at the time of that charter, but it is likely that the burning of the de Redman family's house in Yealand Redmayne during a Scottish raid in the thirteenth century prompted the construction of the original stone-built pele tower and hall at Levens. It is thought that Matthew de Redman, a Commissioner of Array for Westmorland and Lancashire, built the defensive structure whose medieval core still remains at the heart of the present building.

This was a time of border warfare and, although a long way from the Scottish border, the Levens area was vulnerable to attack because the Scots' main invasion route was along the flat west coast of Cumbria to Furness. From there, the invaders would splash across Morecambe Bay into Lancashire and the heartlands of England beyond. Hence around the northern shores of the bay arose a string of these fortlets known as pele towers. Within four miles of Levens there were peles at Arnside, Beetham, Dallam, Hazelslack, Heversham and Sizergh, each helping to provide some measure of security to the district in those dangerous times.

PAGES 12–13
Painting of Levens Hall
by G.S. Elgood, *c.*1900
OPPOSITE The Topiary
Garden: photograph
published in *Country Life*
in 1899

This detail, and those that follow, are from garden, park and estate surveys by Robert Skyring, *c.*1750 (see page 42)

Levens' parkland, which lies to the north and east of the Hall, was enclosed in 1393 by Sir Richard de Redman as a deer park, and although it was reduced in size during the early 1700s, it survives today little changed from its original medieval form.

Levens was eventually sold in 1562 to Sir Alan Bellingham who, it is said, had done spectacularly well from the dissolution of the monasteries. In 1580 his son, James, gained possession and undertook the extensive alterations and improvements that largely made Levens Hall into the building we see today. He completely reshaped the grim medieval structure and added all possible available comforts including a separate dining room, a servants' hall, drawing rooms and even built-in kitchens, as the original pele tower's kitchens were detached so as to reduce the risk of fire. Most rooms were panelled or hung with tapestries, and brilliant plasterwork adorned the ceilings. The spectacular carved wood overmantels date from this era, as do the coats of arms in the Main Hall.

Entries from the diary of Henry Bellingham, James's son, give an insight into some of the pleasures to be had there during a visit to Levens in August 1668:

4th – A Fayr day. We went over Cartmell Sands to Levens and found the sands boggy and hazardous. Reach Levens before dinner, after which to ride a buck but he broke out of the Parke, from thence we came to the Force but gott no Fish. We shot a fat Buck.

5th – A Hott day. We went to Heavsam Church and heard Mr. Ridley preach and the Schoolmaster Green came to dinner with us, in the evening we all walked into the Parke which is very pleasant and delightful, and Tom Banks came to us.

6th – A Hott day. We rode to Heavsam Head and viewed the fine country about. Went to the Force, some fish taken several ways after dinner. Bowled with several of the neighbours. Sweetnam a youth of good fortune, dined with us.

7th – Some rain this morning. We rode and saw the colts. After dinner we went to Kendal where we were handsomely entertained by Mrs. North and her sonne, and by Mr. Joseph Sympson.

8th – Much rain this morning. We hunted an outlyer and brought him into the Park and killed him after seeing admirable sport both by land and water. We bowled all afternoon with Dr Farleton.

'Heavsam' is the village of Heversham, a mile or so south-east of Levens Hall, and the 'Force' refers to Force Falls on the River Kent at the far north-eastern end of the park.

From these entries we know that they were bowling at Levens. They would have played on an open grassy area or green, but sadly its location was not recorded. Later there are references in letters to an 'old orchard' of this era, but sadly there are no other records of the garden at that time.

The Bellinghams did not cling on to Levens for as long as their predecessors. A little over one hundred years after James Bellingham inherited it, his great-grandson Alan, described by a contemporary as 'that ingenious but unhappy young man', lost the whole estate through gambling. In 1686 his affairs were put in the hands of his trustees, and in 1689 Levens Hall and its estate were sold for £24,400 to Colonel James Grahme.

There was a long-running dispute over the value of the standing timber on the estate, which Grahme ultimately never paid for, and it is assumed that this was taken in settlement of an old gambling debt. If this is so, the tradition that Levens was won on the turn of the ace of hearts has some foundation in fact. Certainly the gilded heart decorations found on so many of the lead downspouts at Levens, and thought to refer to Grahme's winning hand, date from this era.

Levens has been sold only twice in its history, each time to a cousin, so fortunately papers and furniture went with the house. The remarkable and extensive collection of letters and receipts in the archive at Levens proves hugely important as we reconstruct the early years of Colonel Grahme's ownership, and the laying out of the garden that we see today.

COLONEL GRAHME

Colonel James Grahme was descended from an extended family of notorious border raiders, a 'fractious and naughty' clan of rievers whose cattle raiding and violence raged savagely across the lawless 'debatable lands' between Scotland and England. A campaign of state terror eventually brought peace to the area, but not before 150 Grahams (as the family spelled their name then) were forced to serve in the Low Countries in 1605. Those who found their way home were deported to Ireland the following year.

James's grandfather Richard escaped exile, and went on foot to London to seek his fortune. He made it there through his skill at horsemanship, wit at court and success in

Portrait of
Colonel Grahme,
by Sir Peter Lely, *c.*1675

business, and was later able to invest in large estates in Lincolnshire, Yorkshire and Cumberland. Ultimately one of the richest of the upper gentry in the north, it was he who founded the family's wealth and respectability. He was made a baronet in 1629, which meant that his son George inherited the title of 'Sir' along with the Cumbrian lands. George was the father of James, later Colonel Grahme, who was to make the garden at Levens.

James was born in Netherby, Cumberland, in 1650, the second child in a family of five boys and one girl. His father died aged thirty-three, and his mother later remarried, and he eventually came to be one of fifteen children in his new home at Hutton in the Forest near Penrith. He went on to be educated at Westminster and Christ Church, Oxford.

In 1671 he started out as a professional soldier, fighting with the King's brother James, Duke of York, as a captain in the French wars against the Dutch. He returned to England in 1674. His military career continued and he ultimately became a lieutenant-colonel.

In 1675 he married Dorothy Howard, one of the maids of honour to the Queen, Catherine of Braganza, and they lived for a while in apartments in St James's Palace, the Duke of York's London home. By 1679 Grahme was attached to the Duke's household and before long, Keeper of the Privy Purse to both the Duke and the Duchess. He was now well placed at the court of the heir to the throne, and his fortunes would be directly linked with the rise and subsequent fall of his master.

In 1682 Grahme was appointed Keeper and Ranger of Bagshot Park, Surrey, a huge area of heathland reserved as a nursery for red deer and other game. Hunting was an important royal pastime, and it was Grahme's responsibility to help ensure that the deer parks and forests were adequately stocked. There are records in his name of large numbers of deer being transported at great expense from forest to forest, including some to St James's and Hyde Parks in London. In 1688, Grahme was involved in the procurement of 108 red deer, which were shipped into Windsor from as far afield as Hamburg.

Grahme took the lease of Bagshot Lodge, a large house where he was to be based until 1699. He had four children, of whom only his daughter Catherine would outlive him.

On the death of Charles II, whose many children were illegitimate, his brother James acceded to the throne. As James II he appointed Grahme Keeper of the Privy Purse almost immediately in 1685, and later made him Keeper of the King's Harthounds and Buckhounds, Alderman of New Windsor and MP for Carlisle.

James II's Catholic leanings, French sympathies and absolutist policies had always been feared in England and he was not allowed to rule for long. At the end of 1688 he was forced to flee to France following the arrival of his Protestant daughter Mary and her husband, William of Orange. Grahme was thus on the wrong side of what later became known as the Glorious Revolution, which saw his master deposed and a new king on the throne. The succeeding years were uncertain times for him. As James II sought to regain his position, amid rumours of Jacobite plotting, numerous warrants for Grahme's arrest on the charge of treason were issued, which resulted in his spending time in prison and a period in hiding. He also faced near financial ruin, as he was made to account for some of his deposed master's finances.

Grahme, however, proved to be a survivor. During this time of huge political upheaval he had the opportunity to acquire the Levens estate in Westmorland. With the fall of his royal master it was perhaps prudent of him to establish a base for his potential retirement from public life close to where he was born and raised. It could also serve to distance him from potentially dangerous court intrigue.

BEAUMONT AND THE BOUNDARIES

When on 5 February 1689 Colonel James Grahme became the new owner of the Levens estate, it comprised the Hall, the deer park, and several farms and manors in the 'bottom of Westmoreland'. It appears that a large circle of friends assisted him at least initially with the purchase price of £24,400. Whatever wealth Grahme had during James II's reign, it seems that little was left following the purchase of Levens, and for many years his finances were precarious.

It is likely that Grahme visited his new property later that year, to plan alterations to the house and garden. He may have brought his gardener with him. Mrs Grahme was certainly there in July, athough the family continued to spend much of their time at Bagshot until 1699, and they also had a house in London. It is because Grahme spent so much of the succeeding years away from Levens, as house and garden were being altered to meet his needs, that we know so much about them. There is a vast correspondence relating to developments on a weekly basis from agent to master, all preserved in the archive.

Little is known of the garden at Levens then, though it is assumed that the ornamental part of it lay to the east of the house, in the area overlooked by the principal rooms and now occupied by the Topiary Garden. To the north there were many elm trees between the house

and the river, which Grahme soon had felled 'to open up the prospect' and to the south there were perhaps the bowling green and orchard. To the west lay wet meadow, and beyond house and garden to the north-east lay stables, farm buildings and the park.

It is at this time, however, that we first hear of Guillaume Beaumont, who has been credited with laying out the gardens at Levens for Colonel Grahme.

We know little of Beaumont's background. His portrait in the Hall, which dates from the early 1700s, is inscribed: 'Monsieur Beaumont. Gardener to King James 2nd & to Col. Jas Grahme. He laid out the Gardens at Hampton Court Palace and at Levens.' Unfortunately, although this suggests that he was French, nothing can be traced of his origins. Beaumont was not the principal gardener at Hampton Court Palace, and he is not mentioned by name in any of the records there. If he did lay out part of the garden, as the inscription suggests, his work was probably in the wilderness to the north of the palace. With the Glorious Revolution of 1688, and the accession of William and Mary, Hampton Court assumed more importance as a prime royal residence and under William, who had a great interest in gardening, a grand landscape was developed to match. Beaumont, however, was not destined to remain there. Perhaps he was dismissed at the change of regime, or perhaps he stayed on for a short time. Whatever the case, he is named in Grahme's accounts at Bagshot from 1689, and by 1690 he was receiving his wages of £10 a year there.

Beaumont's name first appears on a detailed receipt at Bagshot for a large quantity of plants and trees, signed 'Recd October ye 23rd 1689 of Collnll Greyhome by the hand of Mr Wm Beaumont'. The garden at Bagshot was being developed then, and it is likely that it was also used in part as a nursery to grow on plants for later transfer to Levens.

In September 1692, Grahme signed a contract for the building of the south wing and brewhouse, which were to be his major alterations to the house. These were to provide much-needed domestic 'offices' or workrooms, servants' quarters and bedrooms. They would give the house a proper south-facing frontage, provide a major axis for the new garden and enclose an inner courtyard.

Contractors by the names of Cuthbertson and Milburne received £80 and £70 respectively for the masonry and joinery, while Grahme was to supply all materials. Most of these were found locally. Trees for timber came mostly from the park or woodlands on the estate; stone came from small local quarries, and lime for mortar was produced from kilns in the park. Deal, slate and freestone had to be bought in. It is estimated that the final total for building work including other craftsmen's bills, labour and materials may have been as much as £500.

Grahme went south again to Bagshot at the beginning of October 1692, and it is through the many letters of his steward, Hugh James, that we learn in detail of the new building works and the creation of the garden.

The first steps in creating the garden appear to have been defining new eastern and western boundaries. To the east, an old meandering wall was to be replaced with a new one built the length of the garden in a dead straight line. This would necessitate taking in part of the old highway and replacing it with a new stretch outside the wall, where the A6 now runs. One can imagine the muddy quagmire that would have resulted for a time and perhaps sympathize with travellers and Grahme's neighbours.

The new western boundary was to divide the garden from the wet meadow, 'the Aire', beyond. It would take the straightened course of an old drainage ditch, and run from the garden's south-west corner all the way to the river. It was to be a sunken stone retaining wall facing on to the meadow side, thus creating England's first ha-ha. Finally, an old hedge was to be removed, and a new wall built along the southern boundary – the lane to Ninezergh Farm – to make the roughly rectangular enclosure complete.

Portrait of Guillaume Beaumont, artist unknown, English school, *c*.1700

The work on the new south wing and the garden's boundaries took many years to complete, but progress in preparing the ground for growing vegetables was faster. By midsummer 1694, the steward was ready to report: 'The garden is almost stoned and all Led of, and then I intend to sow it with turnips, but first I must plow it over againe' and, later, 'all the Garden was stoned, and I had begun to plow itt but could [get] noe help but our owne horses and have ordered to have it stoned againe for as they plow, the stones arises as much as at first. I intend to sow it with Turnipp.' The efforts of James's men in removing the stones and boulders from the garden soil are appreciated by those that work it today.

Once this work was done, the steward was eager to preserve and collect as much humus-rich, fertile soil as possible – described here as 'moad' or 'mould' – from the garden's new eastern boundary and the ditch to the west:

I will take care about getting as much Mannorr [manure] as I cann for the Garden its been two times plowed and Stoned and now sowen with Turnup seed. I shall not forgett to take all the Moad out of the dich Joynes on the Aire.

Yesterday Beare Finnished his part of the Garden Wall, soe all that is done exsept the places is left to Carry out the Mold into the Garden. I shall gett the Ditch Cleaned assone ass possable but it will be very Tedious and Costly for I must first Groob up all the underwood and trees before I cann make any progress in takeing away the Mould.

By late summer there was news of the Ninezergh wall to the south:

The Milnethropp wallers is upon the end of the Garden Wall which goes as far as to the Aire, and I hope will Finnish That part 10 foot high next weeke, and God willing I intend they shall goe forwards into the Aire and make a Returne and soe leeve it.

Since my last to yow wee have had very Rayny and Windey Weather, that the wallers could not goe Forwards on the Garden Wall. But I am grubing up the Hedge in Ninzer Laine where the Garden Wall are to goe; and if it be sesonable they come againe to Morrow upon itt. I have removed very much good Earth out of the New Highway and hath a Boundance more to remove before I cann beging to make Good the New Way.

. . . as for the garden I shall make all the dispatch I cann I have Cleared a Great part of the New High way, but am Forced to Leave it at present having the wallers to serve with stone, Lime and Sand.

. . . as for the Cleaneing the old Ditch and Grubing the trees it will be impossable to doe itt this yeare, unless it be a very dry season this Michaelmass there have been soe much raine heere of Late, there was soe great a Flood upon Thursday last it was over all the Aire.

There was also trouble over one of the new garden boundaries. It had apparently taken in one acre, seventeen rods of neighbouring farmland: 'Hodgson Our Farmer pretend he never thought yow would take that peece if Ground in to the Garden. I told him he might easelly immagen it wheen he see yow stake it out.'

The steward also mentions bringing stone from a local quarry, 'two Rowelers for your Walkes' and 'Balls for your Gates'. Referring to the latter, he adds 'as for them I have gott a paire of Oxen and sledg to remove them'. The rollers are still at Levens.

In early autumn James's men were working on the walls and fences defining a roughly rectangular court to the front of the house:

> I hope next weeke to Fall upon Makeing the Ground Woorke for the pallisaides walls.
> . . . I sett men upon sawing wood for the pallasaids upon Munday last.

> The Garden Wall goes Forwards. I shall haisten all as much as I cann possable, if bad weather doe not Forehinder.

By mid-autumn, James was worried that the horses pulling cartloads of materials for house, garden and wall work were being almost worked to death:

> I am mightylly put to itt to gett all served with what they want haveing had noe help sence yow went, but our owne horses. I must be forceed to give them Oates or otherwise they will not hold out;

> . . . then I will fall upon Levelling the back Court, and makeing the Walls for the Pallasaides

> . . . our horses is very weeke being soe much wrought, and haveing noe Fogg [fresh grass] and always in action that I must be Forced to give them Oates otherwise they cannot subsist.

He later provides an interesting insight into one of the few medical treatments available for man or beast. 'Tomorrow I intend to blood all the woorke horses, and rest them until this

day sennet [sevennight, or a week] and then fall upon leading stones againe for the dry wall.'

From these extracts it can be seen that the basic outline of the garden enclosure is emerging. It is, however, the coming of Beaumont in November that marks the true beginnings of gardening at Levens.

THE BEGINNINGS OF THE GARDEN

On 1 November 1694, Hugh James wrote to Grahme from Levens to report: 'This night came Mr. Beamont. I shall give him all the assistance possable. You shall heere every post how Mr. Beamont proceeds.' By this time Beaumont had been working for Grahme at Bagshot for at least five years. This is his first recorded appearance at Levens, although it is possible that he had visited before this date to direct the main lines of the new garden enclosure.

Two weeks later James relates how Beaumont had begun making the walks and borders that define the garden today:

> Mr. Beamount begun to worke in the Garden this day sevennight, and is Levelling and Makeing the walke behinde the New building, and Carrying a Nother walke by the end of the house of Office . . . [He] throws out the Good earth, and fills the walke with the Rubbish, and is diging a Boarder all alonge the Highway wall for planting in. The trees are all comed verry safe and well. He intends as fast as he cann to cut all the walkes, and Levell the Ground. You shall know every post as he proceeds.

The 'new building' here was the south wing of Levens Hall, sometimes also referred to as the 'white wing' at the time, probably because of the brilliance of the fresh lime roughcast rendering compared to the weathered dirty grey of the older building. The 'house of office' was the latrine, a small building sited roughly where the present entry kiosk is, and the 'boarder all alonge the highway' was today's A6 wall border.

The soil, that fundamental of good gardening, was looking promising. 'Mr. Beamount is very much pleased with the garden for the Mold he throws out of the Walkes proves Good beyond expectation, and a deep soyle he intends to plant next weeke, or beginging of next weeke after with out faile.'

The main walks were the broad walk running east–west behind the south wing; the long east walk running roughly north–south along the boundary with the newly straightened highway; and the west walk bordering the wet field, the Aire, on the opposite side of the garden, again running north–south.

More trouble with the neighbours over the new garden's boundaries did not distract Beaumont, who was now laying out the 'quarters' or four garden areas that remain a fundamental part of the garden's design. Two broad intersecting grassy pathways cut across each other at a central circular enclosure, thus quartering the large area to the south of the broad walk. Today, that north–south axis is lined by the great beech hedge, while the east–west axis is flanked by broad double herbaceous borders. All still cross over and open out centrally into the beech circle.

> Mr. Wilson of Dallam Tower hath given out some woords as yow and he must Quarrell about the end Garden Wall goes betwixt Stoneyford gate and the Gate goes into Ninesor lane. He says wee have taken up some part of the Highway. I beleive it is soe but its not past 3 Foot, and I am assured wee have left above 15 yds in another place.

> . . . as for Mr. Beamount he goes on verry well with the Garden, and the Mold proves beyond all expectation boath for Goodness and for the deptth of the soyle. He intends to plant in the Quarters he is now a makeing. Yow may be assured he shall have all the assistance possable is to be gott.

By early winter, Hugh James was ready to pass on the seed order for the following season:

> Mr. Beamount . . . goes well on in the Garden and what he does is well done for he Leaves not one stone in the Ground – and will order all the Ground according as yow write. He desires you'll send downe these things as underwritten

>> One peck of Hottspurs peese
>> One quart of suger peese
>> One quart of Runsifull pees
>> One pound Carrott seed
>> One pound Oynion seed
>> One quarter pound of Leeke seed
>> Two ounces of Savoys seed

One Ounce of Collyflower seed

Two ounces of Cabbage Lettice seed

One pound Lettice seed to Drill

One pound of Cresses Seed

One pound of Raddish seed

One pound of Spinnish seed

A little seed of Selearie Lettish. Write all there names on there Papers, and lett them be put well upp.

This vegetable seed order was for relatively large quantities. Either James and Beaumont were expecting very poor germination, or they were planning to grow them on an almost agricultural scale. One pound of lettuce, for instance, would be about half a million seeds. These seeds were almost certainly destined for the open ground of the quarters to the rear of the house. It was not until the eighteenth century that kitchen gardens were moved away from the house and hidden from sight behind high walls.

The quality of soil continued to be of interest, and proved better towards the wet meadow in the west, the Aire, than towards the road in the east:

I writt to yow in my last about some seeds Mr. Beamount would have sent downe. He goes very well Forwards with the Garden. That part lyes towards the Aire proves very well but that next the Highway is very courss. There is very fine Mold where the Sickamoore trees grew which wee must be Forced to Carry in to the Garden to make good some part of the worst of the Ground.

Levelling the ground, by filling in hollows and low areas with good soil, was important. Once that had been done, planting could begin. Beaumont began by 'Makeing the Boarders all around the house in the Garden Side' and planting trees – probably fruit trees – in one of the quarters. By early winter that year, good progress had been made:

Mr: Beamount hath planted all the Side of the New building, and one whole quarter with trees. And he will prepare ground for all sort of Kitching stuffe, and heirbes and peese etc.

Its Now a Frost and snow which I am affraid if continues will hinder much in the
Garden goeing Forwards.

Mr. Beamont hath planted all the trees this day and has planted some part of the Long
Wall; but hath put them all in the Ground, and will plant the rest of the wall ass fast
as the Ground is made Fitt.

Despite the obvious advances within the garden, the absent Colonel Grahme was apparently impatient for completion of the enclosing walls. Hugh James replies to him:

Yours I received dated 6th instant, in which you wounder the Garden wall is noe
Further than the end of the old Garden. The other part is grubed and part of the
Foundation is laid, and the Season was soe Backwards that I could not build with lime
and sand, soe what I did was for the best as I thought. I have fenced in the Garden
that neither Deare nor Haire cann gett in. Mr. Beamont thoe it is Frost goes on in the
Mannagment of the Garden it does not att all forhinder him.

By January 1695, the hard winter weather had set in, and the workmen were relying on short periods of milder weather or thaw, 'thowe' or 'thow', to allow them to move ahead. 'The Frost hath been very Violent this Xmass. Wee had some men woorkeing in the Garden last weeke and this, itt being three days thowe but its now is frost againe which if it Continues Mr. Beamount will be at Bagshott in this Mounthe if thowe not till begining of next.'

There was a brief respite from the freezing conditions. James reports that Beaumont had 'set all the trees and made the border all alonge the new wall and set out and levelled the Quarter over against the new building; here was a thow which made him work. But the worst of the winter's weather soon returned. On 14 January 1695 he writes: 'The Frost continues very hard. Mr. Beamount tooke his Jurney for London this day.' The savage winter continued at Levens with 'great falls of snow' and 'fierce', 'bitter' storms. The earth remained 'hard frozen', but at last the pallisades in the front court were put up and looked 'very well'.

The coming season's seed supplies had arrived, as a detailed receipt shows. Interestingly, it is dated February 1694/5, as at that period today's calendar system was not yet fully in use. Under the old system 25 March, Lady Day, was the beginning of the year and January was still only slowly coming into acceptance as the first month of the new year, so January and February were often given the year of both the new system and the old.

Feberarey ye 19: 1694/5	£	s	d
For 1lb of onine seed	00	05	00
1lb of Carriott seed	00	02	00
1lb of spinedg sed	00	01	04
1lb of drilling Lettis sed	00	01	08
4 ounses Leeke seed	00	01	04
1 quart off sugger peese	00	01	04
1 quart of Rounsefull pees	00	01	00
1 garding Line	00	01	06
2 ouns of sallery seed	00	00	06
For scoch and spruce and sillver			
fur seed	00	08	00
4 oun of Red bete seed	00	01	00
1lb of Redis seed	00	02	00
1/4 of 1 oun of selese Lettis seed	00	00	06
4 oun of sporowgras sed	00	01	04
For 2 water pootes	00	07	00
2 ounce of cabidg seed	00	00	08
sallery seed 1 ounce	00	00	03
witte beete	00	00	04
1 ounce of stock gile flower	00	00	06
swete william	00	00	03
	01	18	10

Along with the requested vegetable seed came a useful garden line and a couple of water pots, similar in principle to our watering cans. Tree seed is also listed, as are those old favourite garden flowers, stocks and sweet Williams. The delivery included asparagus, still grown in the garden today, but the winter's foul weather was to prevent it from being planted for some time yet:

Yours I received, and shall take care to sett the Assparragrass assone ass possable and to get the Ground made fitt for itt assone as the weather will permitt. This last weeke and this hath been very wett that wee could not woorke in the Garden, and this last night and this day, is fallen a great Snow all most 2 foot deep. And a Frost with it; I have led Dung into the Garden for it. All the pallasaides is put upp.

The hard frozen ground at least allowed horses and cartloads of farmyard manure to be led across the garden without getting bogged down or rutting the paths.

Eventually spring arrived. 'The season proves very well now . . . I cannot as yett tell wheather all the trees will take was planted, but some of them doos. If it proves a dry april I shall water them.'

There is then a short, intriguing reference to evergreens: 'Yours I received, and shall take care of the Greens.' These may have been oranges, which were to feature in later correspondence, yews that could be trained into topiary, or perhaps just the firs or other conifers.

In what was to be this steward's last letter, Hugh James wrote: 'I am grubing and Cutting the wood out of the Ditch behind the Garden, which is very trubblesome.' Perhaps he overdid it, for 'on Monday night he fell very ill in his first sleep'. He was 'much out of Order' on Wednesday, and by Thursday was visited by the doctor, who 'let him blood for a pluracy'. But he was soon, in the words of his successor, 'dangerously ill' and 'swell'd about the heart', and he could 'scarce draw his wind by reason a rattling stoppage in his breast'. Hugh James died and was later buried at Heversham.

Following the death of Hugh James, correspondence with Grahme was taken up mainly by the agent, Tim Banks. He was more involved with the legal and accounting work and says less of day-to-day interest about the garden, but in late spring of 1695 he reports: 'Mr Beaumont has ten workemen in the Garding. The Workmen are now upon the Dreine and as soon as they have finished will go with the Wall of the Garding.'

And in midsummer he makes what is thought by some to be the first description of the ha-ha: 'Mr Beamont is carrying on the levell and walks from the new building to the Lane that leads to Nynesergh, has grubbed the hedge that stood betwixt the Garden and the Aire and has filled up the great ditch the brea[d]th he carryes the rest will be fill'd as he goes on so that now the Garding lyes all open within it self which looks very specious.' Apparently 'specious' here means 'handsome', or 'of attractive appearance'.

The following year, in late winter 1696, he writes: 'The trees in the gardin have been dugg about, all the trees and the weeds are taken away; I shall sow some beans and pease which may be serviceable to you when you come.'

His master did not come, however, as this year had proved to be a most difficult one for him. An assassination plot had been discovered that spring, and all known Jacobites, or supporters of James II, were apprehended. Grahme was once again arrested on suspicion of high treason and found himself incarcerated in the Fleet prison. Conditions were appalling there, as he later related: 'There are hundreds of gentlemen now in prison want bread; . . . I can assure you whomever passes his summer in that place will hazard the passing winter in the other world for it is so stinking and noisome.' He was finally released some months later, but not before, in desperation, offering to settle his affairs, leave England and seek his fortune elsewhere.

It appears that Beaumont did not visit Levens that year either, but manure was being collected for his coming, and work continued on the garden wall:

> There has not been a piece of manure used since you went, we have bedded the lane
> with brackens which we will mix with the ashes of the sodds burnt on the Lyme kill
> and Mr Beomont I am sure will find a great quantity of manure at his coming down
> . . . we have had lamentable sad rainy weather for this three weeks . . . It has been all
> this year in such rainy weather that the garding wall is not all done. From the stable end
> to the Corner next Hersham is done and from thence to the Corner next Ninesergh, But
> that side of the wall next the air is not done, a week of fair will finish it.

In January 1697, Beaumont at last returned. Banks reports that he 'Came hither on Tuesday night last and on Thursday he began in the garding.' Much work was done that spring, with between four and twenty-three labourers being employed for about sixpence each day. Weather was bad to begin with – 'we have so great a storme of frost and snow ever since Mr Beomant came that he could do nothing in the garding but lead manure' – but by late winter it seems sufficiently promising for work to begin again: 'This day is the first day that any could work in the garding for the storm broke but on Fryday last we have good hope of fine wether we have bought a great deal of manure besides what was here and led it into the garding.'

The garden was now well prepared, and it was time to plant. Through Banks, Beaumont requested plants to be sent up from Bagshot:

The weather is very good now and Mr. Beoman does follow the garding very Closely he desires you to send downe these things underwritten viiz:t Some of the Double Violet that are next the sage. And every other younge Eiw tree that are next to the violet in that bed. And to send all the Eiw trees that are on the other side of the walk, And two dozen of the Fir-trees that are all along the asparagus bed and a dozen of them that are left of the Scotch firrs And to send hafe a dozen of vine trees that are next the Bee hives but no Frontiniack because they will not ripe here And likewise to send half a dozen of Figg trees and a few Hony suckle and some of the broad Sorrell and Green Sorrell And if you please to send any Triffe to plant the hedging of the walk it must be cut fitt to plant And likewise to send an Ounce of Sweet Marjoram seed And three ounce of Parsley seed and some of the Saffron roots that are planted in the two bedds in the plantation for they are there too thick.

There is a Golden Pippin at the upper end of the garding . . . be pleased to send him some of the grafts.

Perhaps the yews mentioned here became in time the topiary we know today. It is also interesting to see mention of vines. It appears from a later reference that the variety chosen succeeded at Levens. Although those grapes are no longer grown, figs are, and continue to ripen well against sunny walls.

That spring, Beaumont planted what we know today as the parterre in the Topiary Garden, a pattern of grassy paths around flower beds punctuated by topiary. Describing it as a flower garden, Banks reports to Grahme: 'Mr Beoman hath planted the Greens next the Flower Garding and is very busy in doing what is now necessary . . . Mr Beoman has received the plants and things . . . and will have finished in a short time.' The 'Greens' or evergreens are possibly the developing topiary.

Beaumont then returned to Bagshot and in his final report on the garden's progress that year, Banks mentions a 'new plantation', the Wilderness to the south end of the garden. This was certainly not a wilderness in the sense we might use the terms today. Later described as a maze, this area beyond the quarters consisted of a complex geometric pattern of grassy pathways between woodland groves and specimen trees:

Mr Beomant has planted and sowne all the ground that lyes against the new building which was set forth when you were here and has planted the borders round And has planted that part of the new plantation at the end next the Air with Greens and Beech plants in so excellent order to every body's admiration here that I am sure you, will take great delight in it when you come And all along the end of the garding next Hersham he has planted two rows of Chestnuts and Lime trees & amongst them with Beech which makes a very noble walk hee has likewise levelled a great peice of the other plantacion which lyes on the other side of this newly planted [area].

Of the chestnuts, lime and beech originally used in this dense plantation, now only a few old limes remain. Banks also mentions a hotbed for melons and cucumbers:

. . . he is now cleaning all the borders round the house and levelling the ground for the Flower garding; he has made a hot bed and has sowne the Mellon seeds you sent by post & Cowcumbers and has gotten Frames made and glasses. They are come up finely, he does not doubt but they will doe as well here as any where.

A receipt for bulbs and plants, signed by Beaumont and dated 1698

Grahme arrived at Levens later that summer, so might have enjoyed the melons and cucumbers, as well as taking 'great delight' in the 'new plantation'. He stayed at Levens for the remainder of that year, and for much of 1698, perhaps feeling that keeping a low profile would be prudent following the assassination plot and his spell in prison. Beaumont's work therefore did not need to be related to him by post, and thus was largely unrecorded. There is, however, one receipt of interest relating to the garden for 'roots', or bulbs and bare-rooted dormant plants:

Beomants note for roots

	£	s	d
1000 Tulip Roots	2	10	00
200 Double Jounquill	00	18	00
200 of Renunculoes	00	16	00
50 Flaccinellaes	00	04	06
50 Double Pank	00	02	06
75 or ¾ of a 100 Poleanthus	00	10	00

2 pound of double Emony	oo	18	oo
16 Laurell staney	oo	o3	o6
50 Carnations	oo	10	oo
16 Double Rackett white	oo	o3	oo
Total	£ 6	15	6

november the 4 1698
then resaved the full of this
bill by me guillaume bimont

These are tulips, jonquil narcissus, ranunculus, burning bush (*Dictamnus albus*), pinks, polyanthus, anemones, laurustinus (*Viburnum tinus*), carnations and sweet rocket (*Hesperis matronalis*).

When at last Grahme returned to Bagshot to settle his affairs there, Banks subsequently reports: 'all is well at Levens, they are turning the ground over and such work as is necessary in the garding.'

That winter had its usual share of bad weather, and in January 1699 Banks writes: 'All the trees are come but the ends of the Chestnuts & Lime trees are eaten of with horses.' Perhaps they were eaten because they were so large that they stuck out of the end of the delivery wagon.

In the spring of that year, Beaumont was back, working with labourers in the garden, and Banks intriguingly reports that 'Mr. Bemont hath grafted the Greens you sent.' Possibly 'Greens' refers to yew for the topiary, although here it is more likely to mean oranges.

That summer saw Grahme's return to Levens in order to establish it as his principal country house, as he had now vacated the property at Bagshot. Beaumont was also now to be based more permanently at Levens, and Beaumont Hall, also known since as Beaumont Castle and Beaumont's House, was built for him at the south end of the stable block. This building consisted then of three rooms, garret stairs, a fruit room and a cellar, and overlooked a part of the garden that was probably the melon ground, nursery and herb area of the time.

As Grahme was in residence during 1700, there was again no need for progress in the garden to be reported to him in weekly letters, but in early 1701 there is a bill that tells us a little more about the planting Beaumont was doing at the time:

	£	s	d
2 Lignum Vitae trees	0	1	4
2 Laburnum trees	0	1	0
3 Scarlet Honysuckles	0	0	6
2 Medlar trees	0	1	4
6 Laleck trees	0	2	0
6 Shringo trees	0	2	0
4 Snow ball trees	0	1	4
4 provence Roses	0	0	8
6 Damaske Roses	0	1	0
4 Munday Roses	0	0	8
4 Velvet Roses	0	0	8
6 Cinamon Roses	0	1	0
4 Red Roses	0	0	4
60 scotch Firs att 5d per tree	1	5	0
	01	18	10

of ye 10th of Febuary 1700
Then receved of mr bemant ye sum of
one pound 18 shillings Tenn pence in full of
This bill by mr henery wesby his mark

The reference to 'lignum vitae' is surprising, as it is a tropical American tree that we now know as *Guaiacum officinale*, whose extremely hard and heavy wood was turned for bowls; as it does not grow in the UK, it may have been misnamed. The other trees and shrubs appear to be less unusual, and the mix of what we now call 'old' roses would have provided a charming, if relatively brief midsummer display.

By now a new steward, James Loftus, had taken over at Levens. He reports to Grahme, 'bemant bids me tell you that Grapes Ripess very well hear.' Perhaps summers really were better in the 'old days', although autumns and winters may have made up for them: in October, disaster struck when there was a terrible storm. A great many trees were blown down, fences and walls were demolished, slate and thatch ripped from roofs, and buildings damaged. Banks, the agent, mentions 'great and most incredible damage at Levens Park' and Loftus writes: 'I am soury too send this bad newes butt it is such a thing as hath not bene in this Countrey in no ag of man that is alife now att prasent; wind and raine . . . and hath done great damedg in the garden amonght trees; bemun is very much disturbed about is trees he wants stakes for them.'

In fact it appears that almost all the biggest and best trees were blown down, nearly two hundred in all. It is thought that the replanting needed marks the start of Beaumont's involvement in the park.

That winter there was plenty of firewood; Loftus reports: 'when wet days letts the Garden men coot it up in the house.'

At about this time Grahme swore allegiance to the government, a move that publicly displayed his acceptance of William III's accession. It also paved the way for the realization of his own political ambitions, following his son's election to Parliament the previous year. Grahme stood for Appleby, Westmorland, though he was defeated, possibly because of yet another Jacobite scandal: one of his men was charged with high treason, having been overheard talking dangerously in support of the Pretender, James II's son.

In December 1701 Grahme's wife, Dorothy, died following a long illness and in January 1702 he was forced to sell her jewellery. His financial position had always been precarious and he had resorted to mortgaging property and getting loans. Once more he was borrowing large sums from friends.

His luck appeared to be changing, though: in March, William III died and Anne, the daughter of James II, acceded to the English throne. Grahme and his Jacobite friends would now no longer be seen as potential traitors. His finances were also to be eased somewhat by his marriage that same month to a rich widow, Elizabeth Bromley, which would allow him access to her money in due course. July saw Grahme finally elected to Parliament as MP for Appleby. His political respectability was at last re-established.

That spring, Loftus writes of work on what is probably now the East Walk: 'The Garden gos one finly now this fine wether . . . bemant hath Grafelld hallfe way one the long wallk so that must be done too the eind then we shall stope from new woark.' Beaumont's assistant was provided with 'new kote waskote & briches, a hat . . ., one paire of stokens, tow carvats, tow Aprines'.

By the autumn there was news of a developing tree nursery. Grahme wrote from London: 'I sent yesterday by Arthur Dixon the carrier a bag off Beech nutts & another off Acrons for Beomont tell him to sow them all in the garden.' And before the year's end, Grahme heard from his steward at Levens, Loftus, requesting more fruit trees and describing work on the paths, although unfortunately their exact location is unclear:

Beaumont's parterre and flower garden and, to its right, his melon ground and nursery area

mr bemant disiarss you will be pleased too send theise treess downe named all peache treess: one early minean, one white magdelan, one peach off Gattly, one peeach of bellGrad, one Grose mineion, one bell Shenera, one deroyeall, one bourden peach.

Sir the Grase wallke in the Garden os fineshed so now go upon Gravell for the other as wether sarves for it and the walle in the parke gos on prety well according too the season.

January 1703 brought more detailed reports from Loftus of the garden's progress. Beaumont was levelling and laying the Bowling Green, rearranging his plantings and fencing the melon ground and nursery area immediately outside Beaumont's House:

. . . bege your pardon that I did not give you an accounte of thee ackorns and beach nots befor; they waer planted as soone as they come and I thought it was not much mater too give every pertickler of the Garden but [Beaumont] heath movefed all that quarter was made last year the moote of it into the other quarters and bordars that waanted that is thee quarteer whear you say you will have the boulling Green, and hath put all the bordrs in as good order as he cane; he is now moving and altring his

flowars and plants and allsoe hath poulld down the heg was Round the melion
Ground and hath planted the helle bore Round that plase, and we Got very good staex
coot and set Round it and hath Raild and bound it very well; I made the carpenters
cout out the Stakes outt if the hart of a good Eish tree and he hath sown pese benes
and such things as those; now he is upon makeing his hot beds and Leading doung
into the Garden whear it wants, he hath made the hill somthing Lese then it was
when you went he keeps tueing att it we have had very litell frost too houlld.

Sr Bemants disiars the seeds as soune as you cane send them with conveaneants.

He was busy in the following months – in February, 'bemant saith the garding was never
right dongd tell now, he hath a noufe he is very hard att woarke now trinching and digin and
puting all in order that is finshed'; in March, 'The garden gos one as fast the wether will give
Leive . . . bemant Resaved a box this week with tube Roses' and 'Bemant disiars you will be
pleased too send A bage of tuske villets plants as soon as you cane if you pleas,' perhaps a
reference to dog's-tooth violets (*Erythronium dens-canis*) – and by April Loftus was able to
report: 'the garden begins to look well.'

Unfortunately, before the month was out James Loftus had died and once more Grahme
was without a steward. He came to Levens with his new wife later that spring and remained
there for some time. However, he had returned to London by Christmas, when a fire
between the old house and the new south wing burnt down much of the kitchens and
bedrooms above.

In 1704 we have the first written description of the garden by an outsider. Bishop Nicolson
visited in September and noted in his diary: 'The Garden made very fine: the longest gravel-
walk being 360 paces. A maze with Lime-trees, chestnuts, Beech &c.' The long gravel walk
would have been the east walk by the road, and the 'maze' would have been his way of
describing the Wilderness at the south end of the garden.

It seems that the garden's outline and the major plantings were now basically finished.
The enclosure was complete, with a straightened wall along the highway to the east and the
ha-ha to the west. Broad gravelled paths flanked these and were linked together by the broad
walk running from east to west behind the new south or white wing. Against the Ninezergh
wall bounding the garden to the south lay the Wilderness. Between the Wilderness and the
house lay the four quarters, one devoted to the Bowling Green, the others quartered again
for vegetables and fruit. Immediately to the east of the Hall lay the flower garden or parterre,
with developing topiary. Close by was Beaumont's House with his melon ground and

nursery area. Henceforth new works would mainly consist of tree planting in the park, surrounding fields and woodland.

In 1705 there were problems with the ha-ha and repairs had to be made. The new steward, Pierson, writes: 'The garding goes on if all other things stand but the garding wall wheare the great dich went over next to the ayerr was a shrinking outwardss but I got Antony Story & his man and wee have got Three props to it I hope it will stand well now.'

The arrival of the annual seed order continued to be of importance in the garden's seasonal round, but apart from finishing laying and gravelling new pathways around the pallisaded courtyard in front of the Hall, the men turned their attention to tree planting in the park. In 1706 Grahme left instructions 'to have young Oaks & Ashhes planted out of the garden, speak to Beomant'. In early 1707, Pierson writes to him:

Mr Bamount desire yow to send the sedes as soune as posable.

. . . as for the yard the walke betwixt the palestayde and the great gates is finised but noe more is doun now . . .

. . . wee goe on with hedging and sets more quicke out of the parke then thay have in the gardin to Let us have theare is in every Letell gap quickset; bemount bid me let your Honor know that hee wanted mony and the sedes.

In 1708 there were two reports of interest, apparently referring to the planting of the great oak avenue through the park: 'Beamont has Planted to the greate Oake in the spring which is all he designs this yeare; And will gett the Court finished as soone as convenientlly he may' and 'wee go on with the gravell in the Court well and Bemount hath planted to the hy end of the new wall and to the far end of the Ladye Close to whearre the stones Lyes and hath given over planting.' The wall along the park's new southern boundary had been completed, allowing the land outside it to be changed to farmland, and the great avenue was planted inside the reduced park alongside this wall.

In 1709 there is a domestic reference. Pierson writes: 'greatest newes heare is bemount and mary is very kind and cums into The house very ofen.' Beaumont's wife, Ann, had often signed for his wages at Bagshot, but had perhaps died, as there are no records of her after 1702. Mary was the housekeeper at Levens, and they continued to be close for many years.

There was to be other good news that year when Grahme's daughter Catherine was married to her cousin Henry Bowes Howard, 4th Earl of Berkshire, and, most importantly for our story, Catherine began producing grandchildren for Grahme.

With the planting of the great oak avenue in the park, Beaumont's major contribution to the landscape was complete. The avenue was the main carriage drive and route to Levens Hall and, although it did not lead directly to the door, its great length and flanking lines of oaks would have provided visitors with a grand and impressive introduction to the estate.

Most of Beaumont's other extensive tree plantings cannot be pinpointed with any certainty today, with the exception of his innovative treatment of the view across the field to the west of the ha-ha. Here square clumps of trees, later described as 'platoons', marched across the landscape, framing the view towards the wild white cliffs of White Scar in the distance.

BEAUMONT'S LATER YEARS

Beaumont had for many years been spending part of each year travelling to advise Grahme's friends on their garden making, but it seems that from now on he settled permanently at Levens and spent the rest of his days tending to his creation there.

Records from the following years make little mention of the garden, but a few references convey a picture of planting and gardening work continuing.

In 1711 there was the usual annual request for seeds for Beaumont, and later that year the agent, Wilson, writes: 'Mr Bimon desires you'l please to order him some Dung for the Garden or otherwise of necessity tells me much comes short of your Honours directions and what your Honour will expect shold be done.'

In 1715 there was a receipt for:

> grinding three pare of shears and mending a reacke
> one new Raeck and making one how
> nayls for Mr Beaumon
> iron things for a wheelbarrow
> for making the irons for the gardin gatts and mending a fork
> for making one new key for the parke gatts
> and mending one key for the gardin

Also Wilson writes to Grahme in London: 'a Box of Levens Apples Mr Bimon sends your Honour . . . Pares did not thrive this yeare att Leavens soe that Mr Bimon did not think proper to send any.'

In January 1716 the steward, Wilson, writes: '[I] gave Mr Bimon the Melion seed, and have sent your Honour his note for Garden seeds.' Beaumont got the seeds, but 'complains for want of dung'.

In early March Wilson says: 'Mr Bemount hath bene very bad in a stich a cros his chest and could not stir out but he is much beter now and is prety hartty againe and the gardin is in very good order to be at the time a yeare as can be.'

By the end of that month he had recovered and Wilson writes: 'Mr Bimon desires your Honour to buy 3 or 4 syths att London for the Garden, none being to be had in the Country soe suitable as there.'

Apart from the annual request for seeds, the next reference of note is: 'in the Garden Mr Bimon sayes has considered otherwayes for placeing the Greens then building a house for them.' This refers perhaps to the oranges. Other evergreens, such as yews or forest conifers, would hardly warrant 'greenhouse' treatment.

The years go by with requests for seeds and some references to local tree planting, but by 1723 Beaumont's health was giving cause for concern. In February, March and April, Wilson reports:

Mr Beamont poor man is much Afflicted with his old distemper.

Mr Beamont is in a bad state of health, having for ten days had every other day a fitt of the Ague, Dr Archer was with him last week, and will give him something to stop't if it continue.

Mr Beamont is still confined, but the greatest danger I fear is from his Old distemper, which in my thoughts will carry him off in time, but perhaps not speedily, he has got some wine from Newcastle, and wants noething can be gott or done for him.

In 1725: 'Mr Bimon has planted & Cut mostly where wanting And is indifferently well in health.' And in 1726: 'Mr Beamon Often visitted with his Old distemper which he continues to Incourage with Cordial kindness.' Perhaps this was a reference to Beaumont's fondness for wine, and it may well be this that was the cause of his 'distemper' and ultimate demise.

In 1727 Grahme at last retired from Parliament. He was by now seventy-seven years of age, and although he may have visited Levens that summer, he was to spend the remainder of his years at Charlton, Wiltshire, home of his daughter Catherine.

In July of that year there was the first surviving request for a party to see the garden:

To Mr Beaumont att Leavens   July the 23–27

Sir the bearers hereof being part of my family hath a desire to se the Garden at leavens if it may be a proper time to admitt them & their acquaintance itt will be taken as a great favour & will much obleige

Sir your humble servant Robert Hubbersly

they are all honest neighbors.

In December, Beaumont died and was buried at Heversham. Grahme did not live for many more years and was buried at Charlton in 1730. So ended a remarkable era of garden building.

LADY SUFFOLK

On the death of Colonel Grahme, the Levens estate passed to Catherine, his only surviving child. Her husband Henry Bowes Howard, already 4th Earl of Berkshire, inherited the earldom of Suffolk in 1745, and Levens was only one of a number of large houses and estates he owned.

Portrait of Lady Suffolk, by Thomas Hudson, c.1750

In the 1750s, only about twenty years since Beaumont's death, various parts of the Levens estate were surveyed by Robert Skyring, and his portrayals of Levens Hall, its garden and the park are of particular interest. These are the first detailed drawings of the scene as it was then, and they show that it has broadly remained the same to this day.

The Hall itself is shown very much as we would recognize it today. Ladies of the house stand in the fir-flanked forecourt ready to welcome an approaching coach, while the gentlemen enjoy a game of bowls. The parterre is clearly indicated to the side of the house, but unfortunately the detailing here does not include what at this scale would have been relatively small individual topiary specimens; only the yew bower or summerhouse known as the Judge's Wig is shown. The garden's main quartering is obvious, as is a pattern in the Wilderness, but again detail of plantings must be left to the imagination. It is pleasing to see that the draughtsman has not forgotten the gardeners. Three can be seen: one carrying a spade and one a rake, and another pushing a wheelbarrow.

A survey of the park done at the same time shows gentlemen on horseback making their way along Beaumont's great oak avenue. Ancient individual specimen trees, along with fenced and open plantations, can also be clearly discerned. Of special interest are recently planted 'platoons', or square groupings of trees, marching across the parkland, repeating

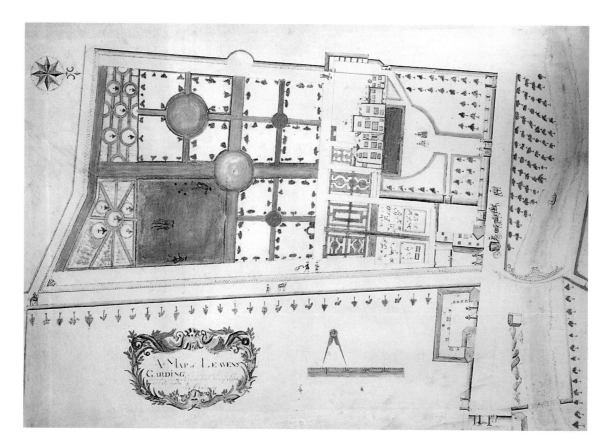

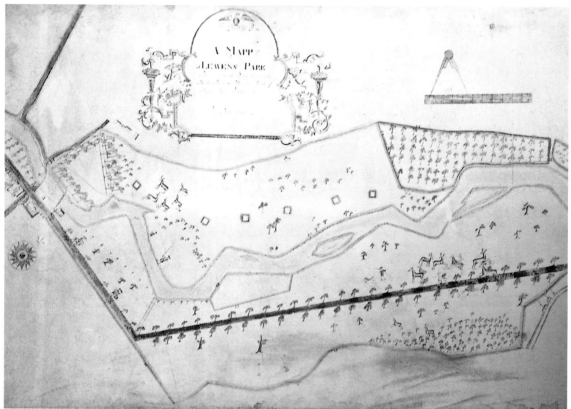

Beaumont's successful treatment of the view west from the ha-ha. A newly planted line of trees along the top of the southern river banking is also apparent. Fishermen with rods alongside the river highlight the park's core sporting purpose, and a huntsman with gun and dog approaches a nervous group of deer.

The owners may have visited Levens at times, but it was not their principal place of residence, and although the garden's formal layout had begun to be unfashionable, no great changes were made to it. If the owners were to alter a landscape anywhere, it is more likely that they would have done so at the main family seat. The Levens estate produced useful income, but with the family mostly absent, there would have been no real reason for the expense or disruption of any change. An agent or steward managed it, but Catherine always took a particular interest in her childhood home, and there exists a large correspondence relating to all matters there.

For some time Craven, father and son, looked after affairs at Levens, but a new steward, John Martyr, arrived in 1754. The younger Craven was investigated for mismanagement and he was soon dismissed. Lady Suffolk described him as 'vile to the last degree to spoil the Beauty of the Park by cutting down Timber he had no authority for'.

She was particularly interested in the state of the orange trees at Levens, writing 'glad my Orange Trees in Health much I Love them' and '[I wish] it was in my power to take a walk in the Garden, and visit my Orange Trees.'

After Beaumont's death, Thomas Tyson, who had worked under Beaumont, had taken over the care of the gardens. It seems that through the succeeding decades, and with the connivance of Craven, the steward, he had worked the garden for his own benefit. Even though the family was not in residence he had kept up a full staff, producing large quantities of fruit and vegetables which he disposed of to his own advantage.

Martyr reports in 1755: 'The ornamental part of the Gardens is in a pretty good Order, allowing for the Great Age of some trees and Mossyness of the Turf, which will inevitably happen by length of time and often mowing if not timely remedied by Planting others and laying down fresh Turf.'

He continues with suggestions for a cost-cutting plan:

> I am well assured that himself [Tyson], one man and one woman with the Addition of
> a labourer for a fortnight in the Spring & a fortnight at Clipping time (that is about
> Midsummer) will be sufficient to keep the Hedges, Trees & Walks in good order, &
> the Quarters or Kitchen Part free from weeds & full Planted with a distinct Cropp in
> each such as Beans in one, Pease in another etc.

Surveys of the garden
(above) and the park
(below), by Robert
Skyring, c.1750

The recent tree planting in the park then comes in for criticism for the small size and the poor quality of stock used:

> the Trees already Planted in Plattoons, and the Line or Range of Oak and Beech that run Paralel with the River on the Top of the Bank in the Park, with divers others were the vilest ever seen for that purpose. Most of them planted about four years agoe and scarcely any of them larger now than ones wrist: The Expence of enclosing has and will be very considerable, before they are Grown out of Danger of the Deer or other Cattle Destroying them.

But he praises Beaumont's earlier plantings:

> The Trees in the Avenue leading through the Park and Planted by Beaumont are surprisingly grown since your Ladyship was at levens, as also the little Grove that was Rail'd off in the Park, likewise the Trees in Barneyhills fronting the House, and the Trees Planted in Plattoons through the Meadow Ground from the Bastion in the Garden grow very well & begin to make a good Figure. But it is a great pity the Vista between them was not somewhat wider, because their growth will intercept the Romantick View of Whitbarrow Scarr in process of time.

Lady Suffolk replies: 'The plattoons are certainly planted too near. Let those come after me make alterations, I'll make none by way of Ornament.'

It is from this exchange that we learn that the 'plattoons' or square clumps of trees planted in the park and the line of trees along the top of the river bank date from this time, *c.*1751; and it confirms that the great avenue and platoons leading out from the ha-ha are from Beaumont's era.

Tyson continued to abuse his position for his own profit for some years. Martyr describes how he neglected Lady Suffolk's dear orange trees:

> On saturday morning there was a great deal of snow lying on Whitbarrow scarr & the adjoining Fells, upon which I offered the man that was taken out of the Garden & Employed in the Husbandry work to assist in removing the Orange Trees & other Exoticks from the Garden to the Greenhouse. But as Tyson could get nothing by this Jobb he Joggd in to Kendal Market and left them to the severity of the Weather til Monday, and in that interval we had two such frosty mornings here as have seldom

seen in the southern Countys were in the Depth of Winter. What Damage they have received I can't judge but time will Discover whether they are to be used as Crab trees & cabbage plants instead of Oranges.

October 1756 brought a 'violent storm of wind': 'a Hurricane was so Great that I thought the House was in Danger of Falling . . . I'm inclined to think there was a great Quantity of Sulphur & Nitre salts in the Violent Gust of winds that Blew down the Trees &c. because the Leaves appear as tho' they were Burnt by fire & Taste very salt as I found by Trial.'

Martyr goes on to list the trees blown down, and buildings damaged. Lady Suffolk replies: 'I am more sorry for the Trees blown down especially the Oakes in the Avenue in the Park, then any other done by the Storm. I hope they can be turn'd to some proffit, as also the Firs in the Court.'

In 1757 Lord Suffolk died, which left the Levens estate entirely for the benefit of his wife. She took a house in London, and depended even more upon the income Levens could generate for her. Towards the end of that year a gentleman offered to rent Levens Hall furnished, along with the garden, park and pasture. His offer must have been tempting, but when it became clear that his plan was to do away with garden and park, and allow sheep and cattle to graze right up to the house, Lady Suffolk refused it. Although she would never visit Levens again, all thought of letting the property was over.

At the end of 1758, Tyson was sacked. He had used the garden for his own profit for too long and neglected parts of it: 'He does not lose a Yard of Ground that will bring anything into his Pocket, but would let the Grass-walks in the Scroll-work of the Flower Garden run rude with[out] mowing, in short he would do nothing to the ornamental part of the Garden but by compulsion.' Archibald MacMillan took over, having worked under Tyson in the garden for the past twenty years.

Martyr fell ill with the 'rascally distemper called the flying Gout or Rheumatism'. This 'wandering scorbutic Gout' eventually got the better of him, and he died the following year.

Dowker took over as steward at Levens in 1759, when he reported: 'the Garden and Greenhouse at Levens look as well as ever I saw them at this season of the Year.' And the following spring: 'Yesterday brought us some fine showers of Rain, which has made Levens Garden look very Gay. I assure your Ladyship that your good old House and everything about it, is in perfect good Order.' In autumn: 'There is now the greatest shew of Fruit in Levens Garden that has been remembered for many Years past.'

Lady Suffolk, the Dowager Countess of Suffolk and Berkshire, died in 1762. Thanks in part to her, Beaumont's creation of garden and parkland landscape was passed on as a whole.

LADY MARY ANDOVER

Lady Andover, from a
painting by John Glover,
1802

On Lady Suffolk's death, the Levens estate passed to her grandson, Henry Howard, who put his widowed mother, Mary Howard, Lady Andover, into the house. She was to remain there for over forty years and Archibald MacMillan was to work for her throughout this period.

There was at the time a growing appreciation of the natural landscape, and linked with this gradual change of fashion came some criticism of the formal treatment of landscapes and gardens that had preceded it. The first guidebooks seeking out picturesque, wild and romantic scenery were published, and though most avoid the unfashionably formal garden, some mention the Levens landscape.

William Gilpin's *Observations, relative Chiefly to Picturesque Beauty, of Several Parts of England, Made in the Year 1772, Particularly the Mountains and Lakes of Cumberland and Westmorland* describes Levens thus:

As we proceeded higher up the creek, the views, increased in beauty. About Levens, a seat of the earl of Suffolk, there is a happy combination of every thing that is lovely and great in landscape. It stands at the head of the creek, upon the Kenet, a wild romantic stream, which rushes to the tide a little below. The house, incompassed with hilly grounds, is well screened from the pernicious effects of the sea-air. But we did not ride up to it. The woods with which it abounds, we were told, grow luxuriantly; and the views at hand are as pleasing, as those at a distance, are great; which consist of a lengthened beach of sand along the creek; and of Whitbarrow-cragg, a rough, and very picturesque promontory; with other high lands, shooting into the bay.

Among the beautiful objects of distance, we consider a winding sand-beach, especially when seen from a woody fore-ground. Its hue, amid the verdure of foliage, is a pleasant, chastising tint. When the tide flows, the sands change their appearance, and take the still more pleasing form of a noble lake.

Levens is at present in a neglected state: but is certainly capable of being made equal to almost any scene in England.

Thomas West mentions the park in his *Guide to the Lakes in Cumberland, Westmorland and Lancashire* following his tour of 1778:

Here is one of the sweetest spots that fancy can imagine. The woods, the rocks, the river, the grounds, are rivals in beauty of style, and variety of contrast. The bends of the river, the bulging of rocks over it, under which in some places it retires in haste, and again breaks out in a calm and spreading stream, are matchless beauties. The ground in some places is bold, and hangs abruptly over the river, or falls into gentle slopes, and easy plains. All is variety, with pleasing transition. Thickets cover the brows; ancient thorns, and more ancient oaks, are scattered over the plain; and clumps, and solitary beach trees of enormous size, that equal, if not surpass, any thing the Chiltern-hills can boast. The park is well stocked with fallow-deer. The side of the Kent is famous for petrifying springs, that incrust vegetable bodies, as moss, leaves of trees, &c. There is one in the park, called the Dropping-well.

Two sketches, *c*.1767, by Lady Andover: LEFT The palisaded enclosure of the front court, looking north towards the river with the stables and Beaumont's House on the right RIGHT A view in Levens Park looking down the River Kent to Levens Bridge

He describes Levens Hall as 'an ancient seat of the late Earl of Suffolk, where a curious specimen of the old stile of gardening may be seen, as laid out by the gardener of King James II'.

Joseph Budworth, in his *A Fortnight's Ramble to the Lakes in Westmorland, Lancashire and Cumberland*, published in 1792 writes:

We entered Levens park, passing through an avenue of lime and beech trees, still keeping the Ken which divides the park well stocked with deer, on both sides. The gardens are laid out in the Dutch style, and were planned by king James's gardener, who resided during part of his master's troubles with the then owner of it . . . The gravel walks are broad and long, and each alley and yew tree has its brother. These are too formal to be interesting; besides, they were the heavy taste of a man that had deformed the beauties of Nature.

From these early reports it can be seen that this 'curious specimen of the old stile gardening', where 'each alley and yew tree has its brother', though criticized, had survived throughout the century that had seen its like swept away in the rest of the country. That the garden at Levens survived is undoubtedly due to the descent of the estate through the female line and the number of fine houses the family held. After Colonel Grahme there was no male heir who might have flaunted his wealth and taste there, and his descendants had more important houses, gardens and landscapes to improve.

Lady Andover inherited a fortune in her own right in 1798, too late for her to do anything much with it, and she died 'immensely rich' at a great age in 1803. She had spent much of her forty-seven years of widowhood at Levens, and loved the romanticism of the garden. Her gardener MacMillan, who was as old as she was, had eventually let things go literally to seed. Everywhere there was 'trailing honeysuckle, sweet smelling mignonette and roses'.

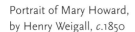

Portrait of Mary Howard, by Henry Weigall, *c.*1850

MacMillan, it seems, somehow struggled on until 1810, by which time he had been at work in the Levens garden for about seventy years, of which he had been the head gardener for fifty-two. A cedar tree was planted next to the house *c.*1780 and, becoming very large, it proved to be a memorial both to Lady Andover's era at Levens and the end of Macmillan's extraordinarily long tenure there as gardener until January 2005.

MARY HOWARD AND FORBES

On the death of Lady Andover in 1803, the estates passed to her daughter Frances Howard. She had married Richard Bagot, who had assumed her surname, and in 1807 her daughter Mary married Colonel Fulke Greville Upton, who also changed his name to Howard, and they came to live at Levens.

A new head gardener, Alexander Forbes, was appointed in 1810 and he oversaw a vigorous re-establishment of horticultural excellence at Levens Hall. It is said that he had to replant 9 miles (14.5 kilometres) of box edging that had got out of hand. His first receipt, from William Falla, nurseryman of Gateshead, in 1811, shows the purchase of 22 box trees and 2,000 yards (1.8 metres) of dwarf box. Forbes later states: 'Dwarf Box for edging is generally sold per yard,

Sketch of Levens Hall
from the Topiary Garden,
by John Buckler, 1814

measuring as many plants as a string three feet long will tie round; and the same quantity
will plant twenty yards of edging, if young plants, and neatly performed.' The restoration
of the garden had begun. It was not just the box, however, that received the attention of
this indomitable Scot. There are many other long and detailed receipts showing the extent
of his annual plant buying.

In 1814, the architect John Buckler visited Levens, and his sketchbook of the time
represents the earliest pictorial portrayal of the Topiary Garden. These illustrations are
particularly important because they are believed to be a very accurate rendition of the scene,
produced without artistic licence. They show the house before the Howard Tower was built,
the young, fast-developing cedar tree, the box-edged parterre as first mapped out by Skyring
in the 1750s and, most importantly, the established yew topiary. These sketches, and the size
of the plants in them, are strong evidence that the topiary is not Forbes's early-nineteenth-
century recreation, as some historians have suggested, and had been in existence and
maintained as such since Beaumont's time. It really is of the late seventeenth century.

There is also an intriguing calendar illustration of this time, again showing the parterre and
large topiary. Interestingly, the house in the background of that picture includes a

The 'Howard plan',
a survey of garden and
park, 1816

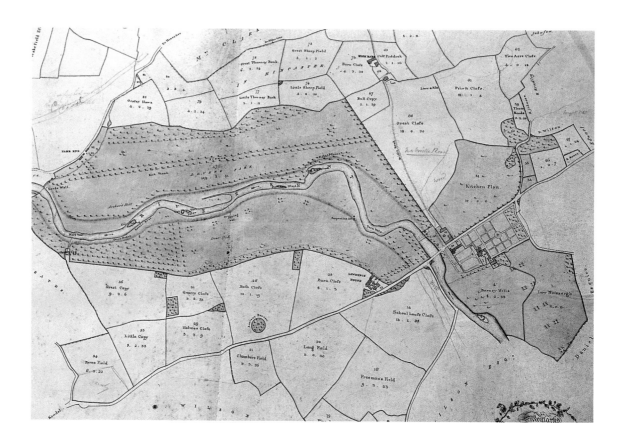

representation of the Howard Tower, but not to its full height. Perhaps the illustration was based on plans for a projected structure, or possibly on one that was by then only partially built.

The estate was surveyed in 1816, and the plan of garden and park gives us an insight into developments since the Skyring plan of the 1750s. Beaumont's quartered garden layout is still plain to see, as are his platoons of trees shown marching across the landscape away from the ha-ha's bastion. His great oak avenue strides out across the park, but by now the later platoon plantings, and the line of trees following the river banking, have almost caught up in size.

Frances Howard died in 1817 and her husband the following year, and once again Levens passed through the female line: it was now inherited by their daughter Mary Howard. The final major addition to the buildings at Levens Hall dates from this time. The Howard Tower was completed by 1820, creating a visually strong corner link between the old kitchen wing and Grahme's south wing.

For some time the head gardener, Alexander Forbes, had been working on a book, which, despite the death of his first printer halfway through its production, was eventually published in 1820. His *Short Hints on Ornamental Gardening* has for its frontispiece illustration a somewhat fictitious but fashionably picturesque representation of the garden, including in the background the new Howard Tower. It does not refer to Levens as such but includes his thoughts on pleasure gardens:

> I am friendly to the fashion of laying out flower gardens on grass lawns, surrounded with a shrubbery of the choicest species, and at proper distances, clusters of Hollyhocks, Dahlias, Delphiniums or Bee-larkspurs, Heleanthemums or perennial Sun Flowers, Rudbeckias, Solidagos or Golden Rods, Starry Asters or Michaelmas Daisies &c; those may be placed promiscuously in the fore-ground of the shrubbery. Walks should judiciously intersect the plantings, in such manner as to lead to the most advantageous points for viewing the flower garden and pleasure grounds.

Frontispiece from *Short Hints on Ornamental Gardening* by head gardener Alexander Forbes, published in 1820

This 'promiscuous' or mixed style of planting old cottage-garden favourites prevailed within the box-edged beds of the parterre at Levens for at least the next hundred years, as succeeding reports and illustrations show. The emphasis on late-flowering species reflected the need for the main display to coincide with the relatively short period each summer and autumn when the Family were likely to be in residence.

Forbes's book includes some useful practical tips about protecting young trees too.

> The best and most simple method of securing young trees, in orchards or in grass-lawns, where they are liable to be damaged by hares, &c., is to tie a wreath of briers or sloe-thorns gently round the stem. – The manner of performing this operation is as follows: – one person must hold the thorns with the brush end upwards, with both hands, at the height required, while another person binds them gently with tarry-spun yarn, or willow-wands. Another brush must be placed immediately below, and tied as before, until you come to the ground. Two men can secure many trees in a short time; and this may be so neatly performed, as not to be any eye-sore, even in pleasure grounds.

Despite the book's title referring to ornamental gardening, Forbes's real interest seems to have been the more productive kitchen garden area. He gives extensive lists of long-gone fruit varieties. That of apples includes the fascinatingly named 'Carnation Apple, Dredges White Lily, Gilliflower Apple, Seek no Further, Embroidered Apple, Golden Monday, Kentish Fill-Basket, Lemon Square, Norfolk Beafing, Oaken Peg, Paradise Pippin, Purse Mouth, Poor

Levens Hall from north of
the river, from the
*Lonsdale Magazine and
Kendal Repository*, 1822

Man's Profit, Red Bag, Ten Shillings, Wiltshire Cat's Head and Wheeler's Extreme'. He gives similar lists for pears, plums, apricots, peaches, nectarines, cherries, figs, mulberries, medlars, quinces, filberts, barberries, vines, currants, raspberries and strawberries.

Gooseberries receive most space. Forbes states that they were 'more various in their kind than any other fruit commonly cultivated', and were given similarly inventive names – 'Adam's Snowball, Anthony's Triumph, Bell Tongue, Black Prince, Bullock's Heart, Goldfinder, Green Hornit, Hedgehog, Honey Comb, Ironmonger, Mogul, Nonsuch, Ostrich Egg, Rider's Hellebore, Rhumbullion, Sir Sidney, Wringley's Melon, White Bear and Worthington's Red Chance'. This is just a short extract from Forbes's recommendations, of which he states 'the foregoing list probably does not contain one-tenth part of the various provincial and fancy names given to this useful fruit in the different counties throughout Britain.'

Forbes was directing his book at a wide audience with general interests, so sadly there was no specific mention of the garden, or details of the topiary. In 1822, however, an article in the *Lonsdale Magazine and Kendal Repository* includes this description:

> The Gardens are extremely fine, and were laid out by Mr. Beamont, gardener to King
> James. A portrait of Beamont is still preserved in a cottage, in the garden, called

Levens from the Garden,
by General Edward Fich,
1825

Beamont Hall, which was created for his especial use, and has been appropriated to the
gardener's use ever since. Some years ago, the gardens were in a wild and neglected
state, but Col. Howard, who has a warm and cultivated taste for the "style and fashion
of other days", has greatly improved them, without, in the least, changing their ancient
form. Under the care of Mr. Forbes, author of an excellent work, on "Ornamental
Gardening," the Levens gardens are justly esteemed for their beauty and tasteful
antiquity. In front of one of the bowers is a military figure, painted on a piece of board,
which tradition says, is Col. Grahame. This bower is altogether a curiosity, and marks
the jealousy of the times when it was cut into its present form. It is of living yew, and
opens upon a spacious walk, inviting the sighing swain to lead the maid of his heart to
its recess, as a proper place to unveil his soul to her view, free from the prying eyes or
listening ears of an old maiden aunt, or suspicious governess. But it flatters only to
betray; for behind, and opening out of two narrow concealed walks, are two small
arbours, entering into the very heart of the clump of yew, and affording every
convenience for hearing the slightest whisper in the large bower, without the least
possibility of being perceived! How many a love-sick maid has had cause to curse these
secret arbours! The bowling green, the gravel and the green walks, are very neat, and
the numerous yews cut into all kinds of grotesque figures, are extremely amusing.

TOP Thomas Allom's view of the garden, *c.*1832
CENTRE From *The Mansions of England in the
Olden Time*, by Joseph Nash, *c.*1844
BOTTOM Levens Hall from north of the river,
J. Stubbs, *c.*1852

The clipped yew bower described here is the one now known as the Judge's Wig. Colonel Grahme's portrayal on wood now hangs in the house.

Following the previous century's embrace of the English Landscape style, and its abhorrence of topiary and the formal treatment of gardens, the early 1800s saw a swinging back of the fashion pendulum, and a return of interest in the Levens style of gardening. John Claudius Loudon, celebrated author of the influential *Encyclopaedia of Gardening*, visited Levens in 1831 and described it as a 'genuine specimen of garden antiquities'. Francis Gibson of Bridge End in Essex visited it in 1834 and noted 'grass alleys and fantastically clipped yew trees', describing the garden as 'the most perfect specimen of the kind ever seen'.

The 'Allom print', a romantic portrayal of the Topiary Garden, dates from this time. Interestingly, it is centred on a minor path leading directly to the new Howard Tower rather than one of the garden's more major axes. And in a beautiful 1840s illustration in Joseph Nash's *The Mansions of England in the Olden Time* the mature Topiary Garden is clearly shown, although the figures are depicted by the artist in costumes from a much earlier period.

Despite some reawakening of interest for the older, more formal style of gardening represented at Levens, there continued to be a great appreciation of the natural landscape. Throughout the nineteenth century, family members would choose their perfect prospect in the park, and waterworn limestone seats were erected in those places. They each bear initials of those who chose the view, and the names and dates are listed in the Levens planting book.

The park was also a favourite subject of the artist Peter de Wint, who came to Levens to teach Mary Howard to paint. Many lovely watercolours of his from this time hang in the house.

Colonel Fulke Greville Howard and Mary Howard also had large estates at Castle Rising, Elford and Ashtead. They shared their time between these and their home in London, usually visiting Levens in alternate autumns. Colonel Howard died in 1846, but Mary was to live for over thirty more years. After 1866, though, it was her

TOP Unfinished view through the topiary, by Peter de Wint, c.1840s
CENTRE The garden in c.1870, by A.F. Lydon
BOTTOM From the *Gardener's Chronicle*, 1874

husband's nephew General the Hon. Arthur Upton who spent time at Levens; he would later inherit the property.

In 1858, the Levens estate was once again surveyed, this time much more accurately than before, and we can clearly see the development of Beaumont's plantings of 150 years before. His platoons of trees defining the view west from the ha-ha, his quartering of the garden, the layout of the front court and his great avenue through the park are all evident. However the main carriage drive through the park has now been diverted away from the strict formality of the avenue, and along the much more dramatic and romantic pathway overlooking the river.

In 1861 Forbes retired after fifty-one years as head gardener at Levens and was replaced by Robert Craig. It is thought that the first surviving photograph of the garden is from around the end of this decade. The panoramic shot shows the Topiary Garden much as we would expect to see it, but interestingly we see clipped hollies amongst the trees. Amazingly, the second largest piece in the garden today, one of the two Great Umbrellas, is not visible.

The *Gardener's Chronicle* magazine featured Levens Hall in 1874 and the article is of as much interest now for its fascinating etched illustrations as for its description of the garden. It is worth quoting some passages to give a flavour of what was growing there.

The account of the planting in the box-edged beds of the Topiary Garden is particularly interesting. 'The beds are principally filled with herbaceous plants and Roses, than which nothing could be more appropriate. Some years ago when the rage for summer bedding plants was at its height, a portion of the herbaceous subjects were removed to make way for the summer bedders, but these are being gradually supplanted by the much more fitting herbaceous plants.'

The writer goes on to list some of the plants used. 'Carnations, Roses, some Gladioli, and an assemblage of other herbaceous subjects, amongst which are a collection of Scillas, including the autumn flowering S. peruviana, S. peruviana alba, S. amoena, S. sibirica, and S. praecox; intermixed with Dog's-tooth Violets and all

Illustration from the first guidebook to Levens, 1878

the obtainable varieties of Narcissus, which must make a fine effect during the spring and summer months.'

Elsewhere in those beds were

Penstemons, Phloxes, Anemone japonica, both the white and pink varieties, Asters, numbers of hardy Lilies, including the tall-growing L. giganteum, Primula japonica, Paeonies, Veronicas, Gentianas, Potentillas, Everlasting Peas, large masses of Sweet Williams in various shades, Campanulas, double and single scarlet Lychnis, Ranunculus, large breadths of carnations, &c. In one sheltered spot I noticed good plants of Ramondia pyrenaica, Primula purpurea, Anthericum Liliastrum, Morina persica, Wulfenia carinthiaca, Adonis pyrenaica, Aquilegia californica, Iris pallida, Campanula celtidifolia, Coreopsis auriculata, trillium grandiflorum.

Further on there were a 'magnificent lot' of hardy orchids – cypripediums and a gigantic form of *Orchis maculata* (now *Dactylorhiza maculata*). The writer also enthuses about the hardy ferns: 'Mr. Craig has a magnificent collection of all the choicest in cultivation.' Free-growing climbing roses were being encouraged to scramble up some of the tallest of the clipped shrubs, and large clumps of pampas grass were dotted about.

Although he describes the glasshouses as being of only secondary consideration, they still contained many decorative plants and vines even bearing crops. There was much fruit grown within the garden itself, and he mentions a relatively new walled kitchen garden across the road as being well stocked. Only the hardier apples and pears would grow there, but the moist climate apparently allowed good vegetables to grow even in the driest of years.

He describes the beauty of the park and river before concluding:

The garden and park with its surroundings at Levens offers more that is strikingly different to each other than is to be met with probably in any other place in the kingdom. In the one, with its acres of Bracken and Bramble, we see as little interference with nature as is compatible with our ideas of an English Landscape; in the other, we find every tree and shrub made to assume some individual form widely different from its nature. The fashion here exemplified came into existence at a period when the principles of gardening were little known or understood, consequently we should not be too harsh in condemning the taste of those with whom it originated. Doubtless there are many who would say it were no loss if all traces of it were obliterated. With this I cannot agree, and should look upon it as sheer vandalism if the few remaining examples of the style were destroyed. But so far as Levens goes, there is little to fear on this head.

Mary Howard died in 1877, the last of Colonel Grahme's direct descendants, and as she had no children, the estate passed to her husband's nephew, General the Hon. Arthur Upton, who had been living there, at least in part, since 1866.

A panoramic view of Levens – probably the earliest photograph of the garden, c.1870.

With the death of Mary Howard, there passed into history too a tradition that had been alive since Colonel Grahme's day. This was the Radish Feast, which had been held each year on the bowling green at Levens, following nearby Milnthorpe's fair day on 12 May.

After a grand dinner at the Cross Keys Hotel in Milnthorpe, the Mayor, Kendal Corporation, tenants and friends of the House of Levens made their way to the Hall for an afternoon of sport and revelry. All along one side of the Bowling Green were trestle tables laden with radishes, oat-cakes and butter, to be washed down with as much ale as could be drunk. It took four men a full day to clean and prepare the wheelbarrowloads of radishes required, and Levens' own extra-potent beer flowed freely.

Those 'colts' new to the event were challenged to down the huge 'constable' glass filled with the strong, dark Morocco ale in one. 'Luck to Levens whilst t'Kent flows' was the ancient toast given while the challenged colt attempted to stand on one leg. If he successfully accomplished that, the crowd would be further entertained by watching blindfolded competitors, all male, fail spectacularly to walk the green in a straight line to reach a pathway through the hedge at the far side. Drunken sports and entertainment continued until night fell and the participants at last staggered off home.

The house and garden were of increasing interest to a wider and more sober audience, however, and perhaps partially with this in mind, the Revd G.F. Weston produced the first guidebook to Levens in 1878. Again, the etchings in this give wonderfully detailed representations of the garden at that time.

General Upton's death without children in 1883 marked the end of this branch of the family. The only living relative suitable to inherit it all was Mary Howard's father's great-great-nephew, Josceline Bagot.

Frank Dicksee's rendering of the topiary, flower garden and house in 1891

THE BAGOTS

When the estate passed to Josceline Bagot, a new head gardener arrived in the person of Alexander Milne. In 1891, William Gibson started at Levens as the foreman gardener, and he took over as head gardener from 1895.

By the end of the nineteenth century photography was beginning to record local life and landscape accurately, and there are some superb images from the 1880s and '90s showing how the garden had developed since its inception almost two centuries earlier, and yet with still a century and more to run to the present day. From these we can see clearly the mixed plantings in the box-edged beds, the by now very large cedar tree, the parterre extending right up to the house, and newly planted topiary developing alongside the originals. The golden yews would have been planted mainly in this century, as would the holly and many of the box figures.

Josceline Bagot had worked in Canada, and some of the maples planted in the park and surrounding woodlands were from seed he collected there. The sheltering woodland to the south and west of the garden was planted at this time and, within the garden, the crenellated yew hedges at either side of the big beech hedge.

The year 1896 saw great excitement at Levens with the birth of a son, Alan Desmond Bagot, potentially the first direct male heir in more than 200 years. This event inspired huge joy, especially as it appeared to end the 'curse of Levens'. This old legend goes that one wild and stormy night a gypsy woman, begging food from the Hall, was turned away and died in the grounds, but not before cursing the House: 'No male heir shall inherit before the Kent ceases to flow and a white fawn is born in the Park.' These apparently impossible events happened when the River Kent froze solidly that winter, and a pure white fawn was born in the park's black fallow deer herd.

Country Life magazine featured the garden in 1899, and included some superb photographs. The detailed views of the parterre, extending as it did then beneath the cedar tree, are particularly interesting.

In *The Book of Topiary*, published in 1904, Levens' head gardener William Gibson lays out his practical advice for aspiring topiarists, as well as providing technical tips. It again provides some interesting period photographs of the garden.

Gertrude Jekyll wrote a commentary on the garden, accompanied by Samuel Elgood's beautiful watercolours, in *Some English Gardens*, published in 1906. The artist gardener writes:

Photographs published in *Country Life*, 1899

The play of light and variety of colour of the green surfaces of the clipped evergreens is a delight to the trained colour-eye. Sometimes in shadow, cold, almost blue, reflecting the sky, with a sunlit edge of surprising brilliancy of golden-green – often all bright gold-green when the young shoots are coming, or when the sunlight catches the surface in one of its many wonderful ways. For the trees, clipped in so many diversities of form,

LEFT Looking down on the beech hedge, Beech Circle and Bowling Green from the Howard Tower, *c.*1900 (from H. Inigo Trigg's *Formal Gardens in England and Scotland*)
RIGHT The River Kent winding through Levens Park: postcard, *c.*1900

offer numberless planes and facets and angles to the light, whose play upon them is infinitely varied. Then the beholder, passing on and looking back, sees the whole thing coloured and lighted anew. This quantity of Yew and Box clipped into an endless variety of fantastic form has often been criticised as childish. Would that all gardens were childish in so happy a way! . . . Why should not a garden be childish? – perhaps when it truly deserves such a term it is the highest praise it could possibly have!

The era before the First World War has been seen as the golden age of the large country house, estate and garden. This was certainly true of Levens, as Charlie Gibson, who was born in 1903, the son of the head gardener, later recalled for an audio archive:

I would think he had ten men in the gardens with him at the time. There were five in the Bothy and he had five labourers, local men off the village.

And they used to start at six o'clock in the morning. Father used to be on the doorstep outside the gardener's cottage at five to six and he used to come down with them and started work at six o'clock. They broke off work at eight o'clock until half past for their breakfast and they had an hour's dinner from half past twelve till half past one, and then they finished at half past five, except in winter when it was dark earlier.

Everything was absolutely kept up spick and span . . . it was a showpiece. But as I say there were ten men in the gardens and they worked long hours. Their only concession, I think, was finishing at four o'clock on Saturday afternoons, and they used to work

Boxing Day and Bank Holidays and all the lot. I think
they got a week's holiday a year, but I'm not sure.

It was a remarkable thing to see those five old
gentlemen, who worked in the gardens, going home
at night time. They used to walk up the path, up by
the beech hedge there with their baskets on their
arms and the stone bottle what they brought their tea
in in the morning, and that lasted them all day. In
the cabin in the yard they had a huge wood fire, and
they used to put the bottles round the fire and keep it
going all day.

Well, in those days of course it was a different life,
as I say he had five indoor men and he had one
almost in each greenhouse and one in the potting

The great oak avenue
through Levens Park:
postcard, *c.*1900

shed. There were heated frames, and there was a vinery which used to produce a
wonderful crop of grapes and there was a melon house where the temperature was never
lower than ninety. The first greenhouse was a big one – it had oriental plants and the
palms. The next one was a miscellaneous house for bedding plants and what-not. And
then in the next one it was all carnations, the most beautiful carnations.

There was a lot of indoor decorating done; Captain Bagot of course had a town house in
London and when the family were up in London during the season or during a parliament
sitting, every Friday morning my father used to put either two or three hampers on the
railway at Heversham station, and it used to be in London the next morning. He used to
put it on in the evening; hampers of vegetables – potatoes, peas and whatever there was in
season in the garden, and that was in London the next morning. Probably fresher than
getting them out of the markets in London. And he did that for years and years.

And anyway, in the season, in the mowing of the lawns at Levens, it was all done by
the horse, Jessie, and she had four leather shoes and we put her leather shoes on and
she mowed the lawn, and she pulled the lawn mower up and down with a man behind.
And the lawn mower would be, I would think, about four foot six across. It has a big
roller on it as well. It needed a horse to pull it; no man could pull it. And she used to do
all the rolled walks in the garden and the lawns in the summer.

They used to trench that kitchen garden right through the winter. It was two spades
deep and all the manure was carted from the farms. My father said that during his time
he reckoned they raised that garden eighteen inches.

LEVENS GARDENS & HALL.

Views through the Topiary
Garden: postcards, *c.*1900

And then in the winter season when there wasn't much to do, the whole of Levens
Park on the right-hand side was raked absolutely clear of leaves. Every yard, every leaf
was saved and put into a heap. My father never used that leafmould until it was five
years old.

The garden was open to the public then, just on Thursday afternoons; there was no
charge. Nobody was allowed to walk around, you had to send them to the yard outside
the gardener's cottage, and wait there. Then me father came and took them round, and
they used to follow him round. We used to get a lot of horse-drawn charabancs. I would
say that on a Thursday afternoon there used to be two or three hundred people through
the gardens. Local people used to come as well.

During the First World War, all his men went to the forces – there was a recruiting
meeting in Levens village on 3 September 1914. My father was very annoyed the next
morning when he found out they had all signed up. I remember Gerald, I think he came
back after the war, but he was about the only one that did. [During that war] he had a
lady from Windermere, and another lady from Stoke-on-Trent, and two or three official
land army girls. And he had them pretty well all through the First World War and his

old men of course; they brought in old Joe Penny out of the woods. He came into the gardens as well.

There are many picture postcards from the early years of the twentieth century showing various aspects of the garden. Most were sold from the head gardener's house following those Thursday afternoon visits. Mass tourism had begun.

William Gibson, the head gardener, left after the war to try his hand at market gardening, later going on to jobbing gardening at Lancaster.

Josceline Bagot had died in 1913, and the estate passed to his son Alan Desmond Bagot. Trustees managed it until he was of age, and amongst other improvements, brought electricity to the Hall in 1916, before which it had been lit by paraffin lamps and candles. Tragically, though, Alan Desmond died of pneumonia in Nice in 1920, so the property reverted to his uncle Richard Bagot, who died the following year in 1921.

The property descended through Josceline Bagot's eldest daughter, Dorothy, now Mrs Gaskell, to her seven-year-old son Oliver Robin Gaskell. He was much too young to make use of it, so the trustees decided to let the house.

A detailed survey of the garden, 1927

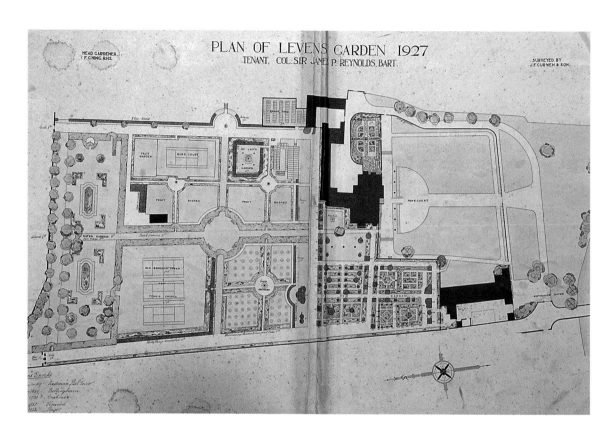

LEVENS SINCE 1918

In 1919 a new head gardener came to Levens, F.C. King, and in the early 1920s, the house was let to the Reynolds, wealthy cotton magnates from Lancashire.

A detailed survey done in 1927 shows some significant changes to the garden. The parterre and weaker topiary have been removed from beneath the shade of the now huge cedar tree, and this area has been put down to grass. The Wilderness has now become an 'Italian' water garden with the construction of two new pools, and a paved formal garden has been created to the west of the Hall. The tennis craze has made its mark with three grass courts lined out on the bowling green, and a hard court obliterating part of Beaumont's original quartering on the west side of the garden. Beaumont's melon ground and frameyard have had their enclosing yew hedges removed, and the Topiary Garden and box-edged beds are extended in their place.

This survey is fascinating in that it shows scaled draughtsman's drawings of all the topiary shapes, and in addition someone has pencilled in their best guess at the age of the pieces.

All the box edges were renewed at this time, and the front court cleared of trees. The framed

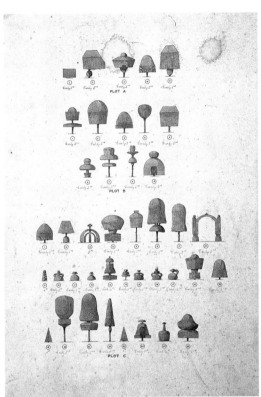

The topiary shapes from the 1927 survey

stone alcove was placed in the Ninezergh wall as a focus for the vista through the beech hedges, and the Ninezergh gate was made.

In 1928, the growth of road transport led to the widening of the A6 on the eastern boundary, and Levens Bridge was doubled in size. The old barn and bothy were demolished to make way for the road, and new bothy accommodation was made above the old stables.

The Reynolds had moved on by the late 1920s. Oliver Gaskell, now aged twenty-three and known by his second name Robin, assumed the name Bagot by Royal Licence in 1936, and in 1937 he and his mother, Mrs Gaskell, were at Levens to show round Queen Mary. Robin was married in 1938 and was now to take on more fully the running of the house, garden and estate.

Unfortunately, though, the war intervened, and Robin was captured very early in the conflict, spending most of it in German prisoner-of-war camps. Fortunately his wife, Mrs Annette Bagot, managed to persuade the Ministry of War to evacuate an order of nuns from Roehampton to the house, rather than a potentially much more damaging billeting of soldiers.

Somehow the topiary received its annual clip, though the big beech hedge did not, and for a time it grew right across the alleys it enclosed, forming dark tunnels. The main wartime activity in the garden was food production, for which all available ground was used, including the Bowling Green, some field areas and a new extension to the kitchen garden.

King, the head gardener, had become fascinated by what we would call today organic principles and the value of compost, humus and earthworms. He had been experimenting for many years, and was certainly well ahead of popular thinking at the time when he published his pamphlet *Is Digging Necessary?* and his books *The Compost Gardener* and *Gardening with Compost*. He was an enthusiastic convert and an evangelist whose message is only now beginning to be more widely heard.

After the war, there was much to do to renovate the garden after its enforced period of partial neglect. The great beech hedge was cut back, and the pools in the Wilderness filled in. The box hedges were renewed once again throughout the garden, and their pattern in the Rose Garden and the ginkgo beds, within the Topiary Garden, assumed their current form.

Since the First World War, Levens Hall had faced financial difficulties, suffering from increased labour costs, heavy taxation and three lots of death duties within ten years, and now more than ever the gardens had to contribute to their upkeep. Market gardening provided the obvious means of doing this and large quantities of cut flowers, fruit and vegetables were produced for sale locally.

In 1954 King moved on to continue his organic crusade elsewhere, and Mr Robertson took over as head gardener. Market gardening continued to be important, and a hardy plant nursery was also developed on site.

Slowly, however, the needs of the paying visitor, now welcome five days a week, took precedence. Part of the ha-ha was filled in, and a parking area was created there to cope with the increasing numbers arriving by car. It was steadily enlarged to handle demand and by the late 1960s about 10,000 visitors were arriving each year. By this time, selling plants with bare roots was being replaced by the container-growing system, allowing customers to plant at any time of the year and therefore make impulse buys. Sales from a new garden centre on the site of the old greenhouses were of increasing importance.

In the 1960s, Beaumont's landscape came under serious threat when the Ministry of Transport tried to build the dual carriageway M6 link road through the end of Levens Park. Eventually, after a public enquiry, for which Mr Bagot employed two QCs to put his case, this now inconceivable desecration was fought off and the new highway was built just to the north.

Mr and Mrs O.R. Bagot retired from Levens in 1975 when their son Charles Henry Bagot, 'Hal', and his wife Susan took over the running of the house, garden and estate. Mr Robertson's son, Brian, inherited his father's position as head gardener in 1980, but by 1986 it was time for change in the garden once again, when I took over the reins.

Gardeners clipping the
Great Umbrella topiary,
using a generator and the
first electric hedge
clippers based on a
modified electric drill,
*c.*1950

THE GARDEN NOW

As one of the few surviving examples of a seventeenth-century garden, the garden at Levens Hall is famous as a unique historical anomaly, a glimpse of an earlier, extraordinary age. But although it is virtually unchanged, like all living organisms it ages, develops and evolves. The bones of a 300-year-old garden may be there to see, but that structure is overlaid by years of growth and decay, and by the efforts of every generation of gardeners to maintain and improve it for an audience of their own.

Gardens can be looked at as art forms, but unlike paintings, which remain static for ever, they are in a constant state of flux. The life cycles of the plants within them – the individual elements of a complex design – play the largest part in this change. Annuals, herbaceous plants, shrubs and trees all play out their lives at different speeds. Growth, maturity and decay are common to them all, but within a garden's complex matrix of life, these interconnected pieces of a three-dimensional jigsaw fade and are renewed on very different time scales.

In the living landscape, trees are perhaps the most static, at least when seen from our human perspective. Those woodland giants at Levens, the oak and the beech, have passed the great age of three centuries, while yews can live for over a thousand years. But the yew trees in the Topiary Garden at Levens have not stood completely unchanged through time, for the topiary is remade anew each year, as it has been since its inception. Through such a long course of history roses, shrubs, fruit trees, annuals and other shorter-lived flowering plants are like ephemeral dustings; yet it is these details that make each age unique. Each generation differs in the way it sees, plants and presents a site. Our perceptions of beauty and the sublime can only be those of our own time, as defined and brought into focus by our own history and experience. Although fashion never swept away the old formality at Levens, it changed Levens' planting style and substance, and continues to do so. Responding to the times in which they lived, the owners of Levens Hall have been influential in that change, as have the gardeners through the years as they endeavoured to create the best environment possible.

The garden at Levens is, therefore, a fascinating place not just because it is old but also because it has been nurtured, cherished and remade through countless generations. Knowing this, we can the better appreciate the small window in time in which we experience the garden. It is exciting because of the very fact that it has changed, and continues to do so. Old gardens give a sense of time, a long view, and a perspective on life worthy of contemplation. And as we look back to the past and feel our place in history, we also imagine a future that we will help shape but which is beyond our short lives to see.

PAGES 68–69 The Topiary Garden in summer: *Antirrhinum majus* 'Liberty Classic Yellow' contrasts with the lilac purple sprays of *Verbena rigida*
OPPOSITE Topiary in spring: fresh green growth on the box above carpets of double daisies (*Bellis perennis* Medici Series)

THE RIVER LAWN AND FIELD

Outside the garden, yet still within its influence, the River Lawn and adjacent field are Levens' link with the landscape beyond. They have always served as an introduction to the site, and as an anchor to set and steady house and garden within their natural surroundings.

From all approaches, you glimpse the house only through trees or over high walls until you finally leave the road at Levens Bridge. The drive slopes down, then at last turns directly up to the Hall itself.

Three centuries and more ago the forecourt was thick with elm trees right down to the water, until in Colonel Grahme's time these were cleared, allowing air and light to reach the building and opening up the prospect to show something of the old packhorse bridge that spanned the river here. This never carried the major highway it does today, but held the undoubtedly foul and potholed local road. The main London route then lay some miles to the east, and most traffic would have sooner risked crossing the quicksands of Morecambe Bay than attempt the local tracks.

Levens Bridge, now classified as an ancient monument, grew in importance through the years. It was widened first in the early nineteenth century with the coming of the turnpike, the toll bar for which stood just outside the garden wall. It was doubled in width once again in 1928, as the road passing the garden was made into dual carriageway to take the increasingly heavy loads of trade and tourist traffic. Levens Bridge became a notorious byword for Bank Holiday traffic snarl-ups in the 1960s before the M6 motorway and its link roads took the strain. Looking up beneath the arches of the bridge, you can clearly see each stage of its long history in its sturdy masonry.

Holme Bottom wood now screens the house from the cars to the north of the river. This is one of the Howards' nineteenth-century additions to the landscape. Originally the public road passed too intimately within their sight along the river banking

Levens Hall from the north, looking across the River Kent and the River Lawn

Levens Bridge spanning
the River Kent

and they had it moved further back. A footpath through trees now marks the way of the old route.

On the River Lawn stands what is perhaps one last remnant of Beaumont's original scheme, the great lime tree. When he arrived here in 1694 this area and its continuation into the field was known as Barney Hills. This huge lime appears to be one of the survivors of the many trees planted here, only to be destroyed by storms while still in their youth. Beneath it in early spring are sweeps of semi-naturalized *Crocus tommasinianus*, their thin and wispy-stalked flowers flourishing copiously alongside snowdrops; later their grassy leaves disappear unnoticed in the sward. The delicately poised *Fritillaria meleagris* can also be found in this moist meadow, along with carpets of golden celandine and the pretty lady's smock (*Cardamine pratensis*). Later the corpse flower (*Lathraea squamaria*) shows itself in the grass beneath the ancient lime. So called because it was thought to grow from buried bodies, it has fascinating chlorophyll-free creamy flowering shoots: a true, but harmless and fascinating parasite.

The huge old London plane is also a favourite beside the river. Much else here is of relatively recent planting, most of it in the last fifty years. The outstanding example is the

Looking west to
Levens Hall

weeping beech. This is an amazingly strong grower and will, with luck and time, produce a remarkable tree. Although still in its youth, it already has an aura of inspirational vigour, health and beauty.

Our aim is to maintain a reasonably clear prospect towards the bridge from the house and the framed glimpses beneath it of the park beyond. The willows alongside the water are pollarded in winter each year but little other maintenance is carried out on the banking except for the control of giant hogweed. This majestic member of the cow parsley tribe seeds prolifically. It is a dangerously successful, relatively recent garden escapee that has spread across wetland and wasteland up and down the country. Its burning sap has marked many children who have innocently played amongst it, and it will smother lesser wild flowers if left unchecked. Himalayan balsam here is the other waterside escapee weed that dominates and destroys the native balance. It is much harder to control, so it is indeed fortunate that it is much less harmful to humans.

The car park is, of course, an appalling visual intrusion on the scene, but one to which we have all become blind; our joy in using our vehicles has anaesthetized us to their impact. The

Sunset over Whitbarrow, beyond the field and river to the west

filling in of the ha-ha's ditch – a historic feature, which, with its sunken wall, separated this area from the garden until relatively recently – and the annexing and surfacing of the pasture in order to provide parking for the increasing numbers of visitors are the price of success for Levens as a visitor destination. A rough guide to its growing popularity is the car park's ever-increasing encroachment on to the grass.

Across the field and river to the west is Nether Levens. Now working farm buildings dominate the scene, but many, many centuries ago there was an important manor house here, almost equal in stature to Levens Hall. Colonel Grahme narrowly missed out adding it to his new estate when he was beaten in the sale by a rival, Wilson of Dallam Tower. It went for just £2,500, but given Grahme's difficult financial position at the time, it is likely that he would have had trouble raising that cash.

In the background is the great mass of Whitbarrow, with the dramatic sheer limestone cliff of White Scar facing out across the Kent estuary. On a clear day, you can glimpse Lakeland's Coniston fells in the distance. In Beaumont's time such country was almost universally seen as wild, inhospitable and frightening, and appreciation of it as landscape was barely in its infancy. He was not frightened, however, of using this view as part of the drama of his design. The bastion of the ha-ha looks out directly to this savage cliff. In Beaumont's day the view was framed by his platoons of trees marching away into the distance.

This field or wet meadow, the Aire of Beaumont's time, contains an old river meander. Perhaps this was part of the 'ditch' from which trees were grubbed 300

The avenue and field beyond the ha-ha: low evening light over Nether Levens

years ago, and perhaps its continuation formed part of a moat for the pele tower 300 years before that. The area often sits in water for much of a wet winter. It is low lying, and the river flows out across it after heavy rain. If high tides join with south-westerly gales, the effect is even more dramatic: the entire area is inundated, disappearing beneath one to two metres of dirty river water as the Kent backs up across this flood plain.

Much of the garden can be submerged too, leaving the Hall barely half a metre above the water line. There is a flood marker stone on which the high points have been marked. The 1800s record was not broken until 1999, but then by a convincing fifty-centimetre margin. In 2004 and 2005 even that record was topped. Either climate change is causing the greater frequency of floods or human intervention in the form of speedier drainage upstream is having its alarming effect with increasing regularity.

However, the dirt, debris, mud, silt and mess that the flood leaves in its wake doubtless serves to enrich the soil, and for most of the time Levens Hall sits surrounded by rich pasture where sheep and cattle safely graze – a familiar and comfortable scene, an encapsulation of the rural idyll, and an appropriate setting for an ancient house and beautiful garden.

THE FRONT LAWNS

As well as the clearance of the large elm trees that once stood in this area, one of Colonel Grahme's early priorities was the enclosure of the front court. The broad gravel drive, aligned directly with the steps and great hall door above, coupled with the fine gravel sweep of the turning area, would have provided a suitably impressive foreground to the building's imposing north frontage for visitors as their horses and carriages swept up and turned before the steps. Today's visitors pass by quickly and in far more comfort, insulated from their surroundings within their 'horseless carriages', but still this area is worth a closer look.

The palisade near the front gates, built by Grahme, is a combination of a low wall with piers at intervals, topped by an ornamental wooden fence. Originally this feature stretched the full length of this side. There was much discussion at the time of the exact form that the new woodwork would take, and of its painting; eventually 'a good iron colour' was settled on. Storm-blown trees badly damaged the woodwork in its early years, and the costly renewal at intervals

Levens Hall, the north front, shown here with Julia Barton's seasonal living sculptures or 'phytoforms', which were inspired by the topiary and the figures shown on Skyring's plan of c.1750

of the less than durable timber may have prompted its reduction and partial replacement by walling. You can, though, still see traces of the original piering in the old stonework.

Trees on the Front Lawns have come and gone through the years. Beaumont's original formal double rows of 'Firrs' were partially destroyed by storms in the eighteenth century. The staggered layout of those that survived served well the prevailing appreciation of a more natural landscape. Conifers, it seems, continued to hold sway here throughout the nineteenth century, but early in the twentieth century all were felled, leaving large fine lawns as the new setting for the house. Now young trees are again becoming established in this area, the mix reflecting the current owners' eclectic tastes. Some of the trees are perhaps transient and may never make great features, but others in time will. Many are just growing out of their gangling youth now, but in a hundred years or more will have matured and have great presence. Perhaps the two matching variegated tulip trees (*Liriodendron tulipifera* 'Aureomarginatum') or some of the many beech cultivars will open a window for future generations on our current thoughts, feelings and attitudes to tree planting.

The broad gravel drive leading away from the house

Slightly older trees of interest include the Indian bean tree (*Catalpa bignonioides*). Last to break bud in spring, usually it only gets round to producing its panicles of pretty foxglove-like flowers in August. It needs something of an 'Indian summer' to lengthen its spectacular clusters of beans before the autumn shutdown.

The much propped mulberry tree (*Morus nigra*) seems to be the most ancient and gnarled specimen on the Front Lawns, yet it is not quite as old as it looks. Mr O.R. Bagot planted it on an early visit to Levens in the 1930s. By late summer it is laden with huge quantities of raspberry-like fruits. They remain hard and extremely acid when red, and it is only as they turn black and are just about to fall that they produce their delicious sweet blackberry-like flavour. It is immediately obvious who is guilty of slyly sampling, as the fruits indelibly stain lips and fingers darkest purple.

The beautiful tree in the corner is the katsura tree (*Cercidiphyllum japonicum*). Its small leaves are sometimes scorched by late spring frosts, and are unusual in that they can sprout singly from the trunk and quite old branches. Its main claims to fame, however, are its superb golden-red autumn colour, and the very strange associated aroma, a mix of strawberry and caramel.

The Front Lawns' side border was established in the early 1990s to replace a tricky-to-maintain thin strip of grass, backed by bulbs. It now houses a mixture of shrubs, slowly going evergreen as new shrubs fill gaps, with the very efficient and virtually weed-proof *Geranium macrorrhizum* as ground cover.

ABOVE The variegated tulip tree (*Liriodendron tulipifera* 'Aureomarginatum'), seen from beneath the Indian bean tree (*Catalpa bignonioides*)
OPPOSITE The seventeenth-century garden: *Tulipa* 'White Triumphator' with double daisies

Over the wall, to the west of the house, lies the area known as the Seventeenth-century Garden. Unfortunately nothing is known of its true seventeenth-century layout, but incarnations through time have included an area of formal rectangular beds within a hard-landscaped terrace, and later mixed plantings within three square grass-bordered beds. In the late 1990s, it took its present form as a box-edged period recreation. It was originally planted with flowers authentic to the seventeenth century, but as the visitor flow has changed, so too has the style of planting, to provide more impact for a longer period, along with reduced

height. The bedding style is now similar to that used within the main parterre to the other side of the house. The developing hornbeam hedge will in time give an even greater sense of enclosure.

Looking up to the Hall, you can see intriguing initials and dates gilded on the lead downspouts. These mark the owners and dates of renewal. 'IGD 1692' is James (I) and Dorothy Grahme. 'MA 1796' marks Mary Andover's era, and 'MCH' Mary Howard's. 'HBS' is the current generation, Hal and Susie Bagot. The building itself was once covered in sombre evergreen ivy, as was fashionable in Victorian times, but this was later removed, perhaps as fashion changed again, or the damage it could do was recognized. The stonework now lies naked,

its rendering picked off clean and the underlying rubble masonry exposed. Doubtless this style of presentation will come to be seen as a late twentieth-century fashion. Time will tell if the removal of the building's traditional roughcast, a perishable, sacrificial layer protecting the stone beneath, was a good idea.

The buildings on the other side of the lawns are the old stables. On the southern end overlooking the main garden is Beaumont's House, and tagged on to the northern end is the entrance lodge. The big stone ball finials on the stable yard gate pillars were put up in Grahme's time. It is interesting that, although we would not dream of doing such a thing now, the first thought of Grahme's steward and workmen was what colour to paint them. Blue was eventually settled on as being the most durable.

Unusually, the way into the main garden area to the east and south is not directly out of the Hall. Family and guests have always had to make their way to it by passing in front of the house to a small door in the side wall. It is one of the greatest tricks played at Levens that from this most inauspicious entrance the visitor is plunged instantly into one of the most remarkable garden scenes to be found anywhere in the world . . .

ABOVE The seventeenth-century garden in billowing silvery white: *Argyranthemum foeniculaceum* with *Senecio cineraria* 'Silver Dust'
OPPOSITE
TOP The seventeenth-century garden in spring, with *Tulipa* 'White Triumphator', surrounded by pansies (*Viola* 'Imperial Lavender Shades')
BOTTOM The seventeenth-century garden in summer, with white *Argyranthemum foeniculaceum* surrounded by *Ageratum houstonianum* 'Leilani Blue'

THE TOPIARY GARDEN

Nothing can prepare visitors for what they will see on going through the small gateway in the wall that is the garden's unassuming entrance. In fact the entrance marks the end of one of the garden's main axes. But it is not that major north–south axis that draws the eye today but the topiary off to one side, across the lawn. A jumble of clean-cut, seemingly abstract forms rising from the precise, compartmentalized lines of the box-edged flower beds grab your attention.

At first glance these inspire a sense of amused wonder; then you experience growing astonishment at the huge size of some pieces and their very great number. The remarkable thing is that no two seem alike, and that the potentially boring, repetitive symmetry of a formal garden has been pushed aside. Smaller shapes intricately and individually carved in box and larger forms in yew, sculpted freeform or as multi-faceted geometric shapes, jostle for attention. But any awe you feel quickly gives way to the pleasure of exploring them and the interest of attempting to make sense of it all.

When Beaumont laid out the parterre here three centuries ago, many other gardeners were making similar parterres at grand houses up and down the country. Levens is unique, however, in its survival. What we see today has not been restored or recreated; but it has evolved through the years. Originally the box-edged beds, set within grassy paths, would perhaps have contained more restrained shapes in yew. Those simple cones, cubes and standard spheres have grown up and grown out, and are now trained into the strange multitude of shapes we see today.

As we have seen, this parterre was planted at the height of the popularity of the formal style, but within a few decades this type of garden had become embarrassingly unfashionable and Levens' popularity suffered with the vagaries of fashion. It was not until the early nineteenth century – when a degree of artificiality next to the house, and also a certain reverence for the past, saw the formal garden

Smooth clipped topiary forms loom forward, jostling for attention

become acceptable again to cultured taste – that this aspect of the garden was admired once more, as an example of an all-but-lost fragment of an earlier age. The development of the amazing array of shapes and the planting of new topiary pieces, including the golden yews, many of the box shapes and also some clipped holly pieces (later removed), incorporated this sense of conscious archaism into the revival of horticultural excellence at Levens during that era.

The parterre extended right up to the house until the early twentieth century, when the shade cast by the cedar tree, planted c.1780, and its demand for water from the ground below necessitated the removal of the topiary and box-edged beds. Partially to compensate for this, the topiary area was extended through to Beaumont's House, replacing the earlier yew-hedged enclosures around the old melon-ground frames.

The box edging, *Buxus sempervirens* 'Suffruticosa', has been lifted and relaid at regular intervals over the years, almost always in the same trenches and to the same pattern. This was done most recently when the box was replaced throughout the garden right after the First World War, and then again in the 1950s, and the parterre is now long overdue for this renovating and reinvigorating treatment.

Most of the hundred-plus shapes are nameless, but as well as the Judge's Wig among them may be found four birds, the Great Umbrella, the Howard Lion, a crowned double arch, Queen Elizabeth and her Maids of Honour, the Jug of Morocco Ale, the King and Queen chess pieces, the Bagot B, and various corkscrews, cakestands, cones and pyramids. It is fascinating to study the development of individual pieces through old paintings and early photographs and guess at their true age.

Now of course they provide not only a great legacy for our enjoyment but also a great burden in their need for

ABOVE Clipping the Judge's Wig with a petrol trimmer
OPPOSITE, CLOCKWISE FROM TOP LEFT The Howard Lion; the Chess Pieces – King and Queen; the Great Umbrella

ABOVE AND OPPOSITE
Spring flowers create
blocks of colour against
the freshly clipped topiary
with (above right) *Tulipa*
'White Triumphator'
and (opposite right)
T. 'Queen of Night'

PAGE 88
TOP Abstract forms
BOTTOM A peacock –
one of a pair
PAGE 89
TOP A golden pheasant
BOTTOM Contrasting
shapes: rounded forms with
a sharp, flat-faceted pyramid

maintenance. Clipping of the topiary usually begins in mid-autumn and takes at least a couple of months. The gardeners use electric and two-stroke petrol trimmers, employing trestles and lightweight scaffolding to reach the higher parts. The flower beds beneath are much trampled in the process, but eventually the plants are composted and the beds dug, ready for a new year's display.

The planting here was once a mixture of herbaceous plants, bulbs and roses. In recent years however, bedding plants have held sway, making bold blocks of colour, like steadying plinths, beneath the detail and focus of the topiary sculptures above. Early pansies and polyanthus herald the spring, and these are often followed by the striking, regal verticality of the lily-flowered tulip 'White Triumphator' and the black tulip 'Queen of Night'. The mainstays of this season are, however, the double daisies *Bellis perennis* Medici Series, whose low, bright green leaves and sharp colours carpet the dark soil. The miniature pompons of red, white and pink are used in single dense colour blocks within the beds. The topiary, clean cut and razor edged after its annual trim, stands out clearly over the bright, cheerful, springtime flowers. The daisies are uniformly dwarf too, allowing the pattern of freshly clipped box hedges to dominate the scene.

In summer, as the year's growth blurs the outline of the topiary, natural billowing leafiness is apparent everywhere. As strong high sunshine or soft warm rain fill the long days, there is a change in emphasis and mood in the underplantings, in the form of taller, looser species, with their colour contribution coming from their foliage or their masses of

individually tiny flowers. These hummocks or pillows of hazy hues seem to spill over the box edges, softening and absorbing their sharp angularity. They produce the foamy effect of waves breaking in a pastel sea around the feet of the great evergreen topiary giants, standing in sombre masses above.

Verbena rigida, with its sprays of lilac purple flowers over bristly twiggy stems, is a favourite here and on warm late-summer days the butterflies throng to it. *Heliotropium arborescens* 'Marine' provides a form of purple too, but in this case, a deeper, almost black shade, through its wide heads and dark foliage. *H.a.* 'Chatsworth' is also grown, not so much for its less than showy bluish purple flowers as for its heady, almost overpowering, wind-carried scent of vanilla, reminiscent to some of cherry pie.

The fresh new summer's growth of the golden yew topiary is successfully reflected in the softly hairy, mounding growth of *Helichrysum petiolare* 'Limelight' and the bright yellow foliage of *Fuchsia* 'Genii'. Antirrhinums are also sometimes planted, as is the cheerful, vigorous and long-flowering yellow daisy *Argyranthemum* 'Butterfly'.

Argyranthemum foeniculaceum is a stalwart, its deeply cut, silvery, fennel-like foliage always dotted throughout with copious white daisy flowers. *Cineraria maritima* 'Silver Dust' or *Helichrysum petiolare* provide useful, neutral silver greys.

Begonias have made a contribution in recent seasons, but not the dwarf, gaudy, bright-coloured *semperflorens* type, nor the monstrous double-flowered 'Non Stop' cultivars.

PAGE 92 Spring bedding
TOP Underplanting of pansies (*Viola* 'Imperial Lavender Shades')
BOTTOM A carpet of double daisies (*Bellis perennis* Medici Series) in red and white
PAGE 93 Summer bedding
TOP LEFT *Verbena* 'Sterling Star'
TOP RIGHT *Antirrhinum majus* 'Liberty Classic Yellow' surrounding beds of *Verbena rigida*
BOTTOM Dark-foliaged *Heliotropium arborescens* 'Marine' to the left and the yellow daisy-flowered *Argyranthemum* 'Butterfly' to the right; *Helichrysum petiolare* 'Limelight' and *Verbena rigida* to the rear

At Levens, the larger, looser, small-flowered *Begonia* Inferno Series proves more in keeping. Various foliage-effect fuchsias, stocks, verbenas and nicotianas have also played their part over the years.

The exciting thing is that the display is never the same two years running. We are continually trialling new plants, and those that help create the perfect picture we grow again. This is a garden like no other for visual effect. The sight of tightly trimmed evergreens set in a sea of flowers has huge impact and the parterre is gardened to emphasize and enhance that moment.

To one side, yet still within the shadow of the topiary, distinct in its planting, is the Rose Garden. This area has been defined as such for the best part of the last one hundred years, though the present box-edged bed pattern is from the 1950s. Roses have always played their part at Levens since Beaumont planted 'Provence Roses, Damaske Roses, Munday Roses, Velvet Roses, Cinamon Roses, and Red Roses' over 300 years ago. In the nineteenth century it was reported that newer, perhaps more tender varieties, were regularly partially lifted (dug from the ground and then replaced) each autumn, so as to check their growth and prevent an early spring flush being caught by late frosts.

The post-war plantings here were sick and dwindling by the late 1980s, and so they were

TOP The rose garden, with the two giant chess pieces guarding Beaumont's House in the background
BOTTOM A heady mixture of David Austin's English roses

all grubbed up. The rose-sick soil was replaced with fresh, to a depth of at least half a metre, and we planted David Austin's English roses in mixed groupings throughout. These are the result of a relatively recent breeding programme to bring out something of the scent, colour and flower form of old roses, while introducing new repeat-flowering capabilities.

The Rose Garden reaches a peak at midsummer with its first great flush of flowers, but with careful deadheading, feeding and a mild autumn, there are blooms right through till early winter. Hard pruning in late winter creates some form of orderliness, and this is effective early in the season in allowing the outlines of box and yew to dominate. As spring turns into summer, though, the roses' sprawling, twiggy, lax or upright natural growth takes over. Although this may seem to detract from the sculpted lines of the Topiary Garden, all is forgiven on pressing one's nose into the velvety softness of a fully open flower and breathing in the heady perfume. The roses' colour and form are certainly attractive, but it is their scent that intoxicates and wins over the visitor. Each variety is subtly different, and it is a wonderful, indulgent experience to go from open flower to flower, drinking deeply of their individual and distinct charms. Old rose and tea rose notes are

The rose garden, seen from beneath the maidenhair tree (*Ginkgo biloba*)

The heavily textured trunk of the dawn redwood (*Metasequoia glyptostroboides*), contrasting with the topiary around it

obvious, but there may also be hints of warm clove, honey, myrrh and musk, deliciously fruity raspberry, strawberry, apple, peach and apricot, or cooler lemons and violet.

The varieties here include the evocatively named 'Eglantyne', 'Mary Rose', 'Perdita', 'Gertrude Jekyll', 'Brother Cadfael', 'Winchester Cathedral', 'The Countryman', 'Redoute', 'William Morris', 'Wenlock', 'Francine Austin', 'English Garden', 'L.D. Braithwaite' and 'Belle Story'. Underplantings were tried here, but although wonderful in themselves, we rejected them as competing with the roses to their detriment, distracting from the area's main focus. Now it is simply roses, all mingled together in a charming 'old-fashioned' mixture in which the beauty of these flowers is the single theme.

The maidenhair tree (*Ginkgo biloba*) in the central bed was planted during the 1950s when this area was renewed. Unusually, this is a deciduous conifer that bears broad rather than needle-like leaves. It is the sole survivor of an ancient plant family better known through their fossil record. Apparently it is much used as a street tree in its native China, where the fruit is something of a delicacy. Here it provides interest value and is highly ornamental in autumn, when its foliage turns a glowing yellow before dropping to form heavy smothering sheets on the ground below. The other, slightly larger ginkgo near by was planted about 1900.

The third large tree placed like the others rather incongruously within this area of the Topiary Garden is a dawn redwood (*Metasequoia glyptostroboides*). This is another deciduous conifer with lovely autumn colour. The species was only discovered in China in 1941, and the example planted here in the early 1950s has quickly grown into a superb large tree. Its delicate, lacy, fern-like foliage and sweeping, weeping, curtain-like branches are truly beautiful, and a pleasant contrast to the clipped yew and box. But this is only a relatively young specimen. In time it will grow to three or four times its current size, dominating and destroying the garden beneath, as the cedar did nearer to the house. Planted perhaps to commemorate births, events or anniversaries, or maybe just as memorials to the late-twentieth century's obsession with plantsmanship, these trees have grown into large trees quite unsuited to their situation. They are potentially physically damaging to the far older topiary and also aesthetically harmful, for although they are individually magnificent, their form of beauty is alien within this context. Let us hope that they will be removed before the topiary and parterre below deteriorates and their removal instead becomes inevitable.

This area is separated from the rest of the garden to the south by thick old hedges of crenellated yew, which have been cut back hard in recent years to rejuvenate and restore them. In summer they are partially smothered with the Scottish flame flower (*Tropaeolum speciosum*), a herbaceous climber that scrambles up the hedge surface each year, clinging on with its twisting leaf petioles. It produces countless small scarlet nasturtium-like flowers, in bright contrast to the darkness of the yew, followed by amazing blue seeds. It is certainly attractive, and seems to thrive here – so much so that it denies the hedge leaves full daylight and the hedge would end up damaged and dying if it were not for a bit of judicious thinning from time to time.

It is the topiary, however, that is at the heart of the experience here, and the feeling of being linked in some way with the past as you absorb the atmosphere of bygone ages in a garden that has been tended for over 300 years. It is true that forest trees or even human architecture can be of a similar age, but these do not convey the same sense of time passed. Here the yew and box has been trimmed and crafted with care year in year out, for longer than anyone can possibly remember. It is because of this human link, and the intimate scale of the garden, that these larger-than-life sculpted green figures evoke in us empathy with an earlier age.

Old hedges of crenellated yew with Scottish flame flower (*Tropaeolum speciosum*); the emerging fountain of silvery foliage in front is *Salix alba* var. *sericea*

WALL BORDERS

The walling and building stone at Levens Hall was the native fractured limestone bedrock. It was taken from nearby shallow quarries in the park or the ice house woods to the south-east of the garden, on the other side of the A6, and carted the few hundred metres to where it was used. Lime for the mortar was burnt in the kilns in the park, or at High Barns, just a stone's throw away. Cement, a relatively recent innovation, only came into widespread use here as a mortar ingredient during the twentieth century. Although effective, its hard, tenacious and unyielding nature may well be a matter of regret for future generations.

The garden walls appear almost dazzlingly bright white in strong hard sunlight, but they mellow to light grey when reflecting cloud, or darken still further under the leaden, rain-filled skies of winter. They were never built dry with a batter for stability, but from the start were mortared and had vertical sides. After so long, they are showing signs of their age in many places, and they are patched or rebuilt in sections as storm, wind and rain demolish them. As the lime

Actinidia kolomikta with its striking foliage colour

mortar crumbles and loosens and the stone shatters as a result of frost, small plants begin to colonize. Among the native plants clinging to life on the walls is the pretty little ivy-leaved toadflax (*Cymbalaria muralis*), which can be found in flower for much of the year. Those tough and wiry ferns, the maidenhair spleenwort (*Asplenium trichomanes*) and wall rue (*A. ruta-muraria*) can be found almost everywhere too, whilst their larger, broader-leaved cousin the hart's tongue fern (*A. scolopendrium*) favours the darker, danker areas at the base of the stonework. As rotting leaf litter and crumbling rock turn to soil, grasses, nipplewort and other herbage move in.

Fortunately, though, most of the walls are still sound enough to support more exotic items of horticultural interest, and the sheltered borders beneath them contain many gems.

One of the most commented-upon climbers is the striking *Actinidia kolomikta*, present in the borders in a number of places. If its tender young leaves escape cutting by late spring frosts, they go on to show bold splashes of pink tipped with white, which have a brighter and longer-lasting effect than any flowers. Its unlikely relative *A. chinensis*, the Chinese gooseberry or kiwi fruit, is also here as an ornamental, always looking for more room to fling its long, bristlingly hairy tentacles.

Contrasting yellow and purple: *Cornus alba* 'Aurea' with *Hydrangea aspera* subsp. *sargentiana* and *Sambucus nigra* 'Guincho Purple'

ABOVE The wisteria on
Beaumont's House
OPPOSITE Looking over
the grey border towards
the long wall border,
where yellow and purple
themes unite the planting

The lacecap hydrangeas, *H. aspera*, *H.a.* Villosa Group, and *H.a.* subsp. *sargentiana*, are well represented. Despite having their first tender shoots trashed by late frosts on an annual basis, they always go on to produce a superb flowering display of their characteristic flat heads surrounded by small dancing outer florets. In the case of *H. aspera* these are huge, and well matched to this gaunt shrub's enormous felted leaves.

There are many examples of wisteria too. None is finer than that growing up Beaumont's House. We are gradually coaxing its long twining shoots across the front of the house from its origins on the nearby wall, and in time it will cover the entire gable end with its superb exhibition of scented, lilac-blue, hanging flower clusters. The white-flowered form in the corner near here has escaped the confines of the wall and hoisted itself right to the top of the large nearby lime tree, which has resulted in a very confusing flower display.

In spring, billowing clouds of sweet vanilla aroma waft across the garden from *Azara microphylla*, its tiny insignificant flowers giving no hint that they are the source of this most powerful and heady scent. In summer, among much else, the buddlejas, including the slightly tender *B. crispa*, prove a big draw for the butterflies. And by autumn, the huge leaves of *Vitis cognetiae* have spread far, colouring brilliantly before their fall.

The longest straight wall and border is that along the garden's eastern boundary, which defines and protects the garden from the rush of the busy road and the reality of the world outside. It is the visual impact of the planting here that is of prime importance. A yellow and purple theme is gradually emerging, and these repeated colour associations give this long feature great unity. Gold is provided by repeated groupings of *Cornus alba* 'Aurea', *Hedera canariensis* 'Gloire de Marengo', *Philadelphus coronarius* 'Aureus' and their like. Purple is provided by the excellent *Vitis vinifera* 'Purpurea', *Sambucus nigra* 'Guincho Purple', *Berberis thunbergii* f. *atropurpurea* and many others.

In times gone by this long border would have contained espaliered fruit from end to end, but now it is gardened for aesthetic effect rather than food. It is an example of how, as times change, the garden's style and planting have evolved to serve the needs of fresh audiences. Since it was originally designed for fruit, it is a little narrow for the natural sprawl of many shrubs. We prune these back in late winter and give them a deep leaf-litter mulch. This is one of the most striking, yet low-maintenance, features at Levens.

THE ORCHARD AND ORCHARD BORDERS

The garden at Levens is fortunate in being compartmentalized by its quartered design and the ancient hedges that divide and form its layout, to make a series of discrete areas that can offer quite differing themes.

As you move away from the overgrown and eccentric formality of the topiary area, you can glimpse through peepholes in the crenellated hedge a different world, a looser, more natural garden. This is the Orchard, where narrow grass pathways lead through mixed borders overflowing with flowers.

The older fruit trees here were planted in the early 1900s and include 'Nelson's Favourite', 'Duchess of Bedford', 'Kings Acre Bountiful', 'Wealthy', 'King of the Pippins', 'Baron Wolsey', 'Norfolk Beauty', 'Lady Sudely', 'Lord Lambourne' and many others. More recently, various quinces, medlars and damsons have been added to further increase the diversity. All have been placed on the rigid square grid of the original plantings.

In spring, bold, square blocks of the tulip 'Apeldoorn' create a pattern of vivid colour beneath the trees. One of the most vigorous Darwin hybrids, this tulip can cope

LEFT *Tulipa* 'Apeldoorn' provides welcome shots of colour against the green
RIGHT Fruit trees laid out in a rigid grid pattern. As the tulip flowers fade, longer grass and wild flowers replace them to sustain the chequerboard effect

successfully with the competition provided by the grass. Its huge red flowers are in bright contrast to the fresh greens of the newly emerging leaves all around. As they open wide in the late spring sunshine, the detail of their striking yellow and black interiors is revealed. When finally their petals drop, the focus falls upon the trees above as they are all too fleetingly smothered in pink and white blossom.

Though once seriously cultivated for the crop they could provide, the fruit trees are now purely ornamental. The grass beneath them is mowed to an interesting grid pattern, with longer squares beneath the trees in late spring to allow the tulips' fading foliage to replenish the bulbs' stores for the following year. The longer grass is then cut back, before being allowed to grow up again to create a fascinating visual effect of shadow, light and texture.

The lovely mixture of herbaceous ground cover plants spilling out across the grassy walkways between the double borders is punctuated at intervals by matching shrubs reflecting each other across the paths. Of these, the silver willow *Salix alba* var. *sericea* is the most striking, a three-metre fountain of silver-grey narrow leaves shooting up from the annually pollarded club-like stumps. Alternating with the willow are pairings of *Cotinus coggygria* 'Royal Purple', their dark orb-like leaves bubbling up to make a colourful contrast.

The circular centre to this garden quarter is a bright, light-filled space. This is emphasized by the dominant enclosing plantings of the white-variegated *Cornus alba* 'Elegantissima' and the ground cover of the silvery grey *Stachys byzantina*. The central urn carries on this theme with a mound of the variegated scented *Pelargonium* 'Lady Plymouth' and cascading trails of *Plectranthus madagascariensis* 'Variegated Mintleaf'.

The Orchard and its borders are possibly the most relaxed and intimate of Levens' many distinct garden areas and offer a pleasing contrast to the box-edged geometry that precedes them.

LEFT The orchard borders in spring: (top) fresh green hummocks of foliage; (bottom) a silvery grey fountain of foliage beginning to emerge from the pollarded clubs of *Salix alba* var. *sericea*
RIGHT The central circular space in the orchard borders, where light, white and variegated plantings dominate

THE BOWLING GREEN

The game of bowls has been popular in England for many centuries, as have, in years gone by, the drunkenness and gambling that went with it. In fact, it was so popular that a law was once passed banning it because it caused people to neglect their compulsory archery practice. This rule did not, however, extend to the rich, who could be licensed to continue the game unhindered.

The Bellinghams were certainly playing bowls at Levens in the 1600s, before Colonel Grahme took over and had the garden laid out, ensuring that one full 'quarter' was devoted to a green. The gardeners of old did not have our modern machine mowers, but would have scythed the grass every fortnight. They would have knocked lumps and bumps into place with wooden 'beaters' and if the sward became too mossy they would have lifted it and replaced it with fresh turf from the meadow.

The old bowls used in Colonel Grahme's time were still in play there until the early years of the twentieth century, when bowls gave way to tennis, which had become hugely fashionable amongst the 'country house set', and three grass courts were marked out on the old green. In the 1940s everything was cleared away for the war effort, when the 'Dig for Victory' campaign saw all available land in use for fruit and vegetable growing. This area was ploughed and put into production, but it was not much good, the turf having originally been laid on a firm and fast-draining stone, gravel and ash base.

After the war the area was never quite the same again. As most effort on site was being put into making Levens commercially viable through market gardening and as a visitor attraction, maintenance was minimal. The grass was allowed to grow long and rough for some time, but in the early 1990s it was renovated. Dozens of trailerloads of moss and thatch were removed, the fertility of the soil increased and the weeds controlled. Today the mellow knock of wood on wood can again be heard, as bowls are once more played upon the

A game of croquet on the Bowling Green

The Bowling Green,
looking towards the
Orchard: foaming clouds
of *Crambe cordifolia* rise
from the rear of the
flanking Pastel Border

green, and in summer the relatively new, deceptively genteel yet highly competitive game of croquet is played.

The green today is far from the flat or slightly raised crown demanded by modern bowls players. Its large size and slightly undulating surface make for interesting play, though, and there are a few other surprises for those new to it. Hidden amongst the sward are a number of ball-swallowing drop holes. During the summer, mice and voles move into these underground channels, enlarging invisible pitfalls for the unwary. After heavy rain they form natural springs from which water bubbles up. Every few years, storms create deluges so great that the pressurized underground water cannot escape fast enough, and the turf lifts in giant wobbling hummocks like a series of rounded water beds. Although the hummocks persist alarmingly for a few days, in time they sink back into place once more, to the relief of all.

Many years ago this area would have been a very private one, enclosed as it still is on two sides by the thick walls of the beech hedge and on the other two sides by the impenetrable faces of holly hedges, which had pointed tops with decorative standards rising at intervals along their length. The beech hedge remains, but the holly hedges were removed in the mid-twentieth century to make way for the double herbaceous borders to the north and a narrow, raised iris border to the east.

The bearded iris cultivars were beautiful when in flower, but for the other fifty weeks of the year provided no return for their high-maintenance needs. They were removed in the late 1980s, and replaced by low-growing grey foliage plants. Although often dank and drab after

a wet winter, these plants provide much of interest through spring, summer and autumn. From the mounds of the delicately divided silver leaves of *Artemisia* 'Powis Castle' to the white felted leaves and pink-eyed flowers of the biennial dusty miller, *Lychnis coronaria* 'Oculata'; from the long-stalked daisy flowers and cut, grey leaves of *Anthemis punctata* subsp. *cupaniana* to the vigorous, glaucous foliage and perennial purple flowers of *Erysimum* 'Bowles's Mauve', all is unity through shared foliage tone. The two most dramatic contributions come, however, from vertical accents. The softly spiky, blue-grey rosettes of *Kniphofia caulescens,* topped with pokers of burning orange in mid-autumn, never fail to excite; nor do the white-felted candelabra of the biennial *Verbascum* 'Arctic Summer'.

In part to echo this grey theme, and in part for the sake of the excellent and long-lasting effect they create, the Bowling Green is flanked on the two bordered sides by long belts of catmint, *Nepeta* 'Six Hills Giant'. This tough and underrated perennial produces fountains of greyish foliage topped with bee-and-butterfly-beloved flowers of lavender blue in abundance. As the first big flush of flowers fade, new sprays rise up from the opening crowns and continue the display till autumn.

The Bowling Green is the largest open lawn at Levens, and provides a welcome change from the horticultural 'hits' elsewhere. It is good to remember that the pleasures of an English garden can include fun and games and not just flower, fruit and form.

The velvety green surface of the Bowling Green is surrounded by the massive walls of the beech hedge and broad belts of catmint (*Nepeta* 'Six Hills Giant')

THE PASTEL BORDERS

The broad grass paths running east to west across the garden have always formed one of its major axes. From the east they cross the great Beech Circle, and continue on across the ha-ha's bastion to the avenue and landscape beyond. They cut the garden in two and the crossing beech hedge walks further dissect it into quarters. The Beech Circle also serves to divide and separate the main walks and their plantings so as to allow an interesting variation of atmosphere and emphasis.

To the east the double herbaceous borders lining the east–west walk are unified by a pastel colour scheme. Pink, blue and yellow flowers all find a place here, generally in their lighter tones, along with cream and white. In some ways, when describing a colour theme, it is easiest to say which colours are excluded, and here those are the harder reds, oranges, deep blues, dark purples and strong yellows.

Wood and wire pyramids placed at regular intervals provide form and height early in the season. Matched pairs of Viticella clematis cultivars fly up these supports in spring after their hard winter pruning. From late summer they are smothered by masses of tiny nodding light

purple, pink and mauve flowers, providing charming punctuation along the walk. Varieties include 'Blue Belle', 'Minuet', 'Huldine', 'Mrs T. Lundell', 'Abundance' and 'Grandiflora Sanguinea'. Old-fashioned sweet peas, placed to run up the back of these structures, give further fragrant delight.

Mainstays of the early herbaceous display include the low-growing, rosy-hyacinth-like flowers of *Stachys macrantha* 'Rosea' and the sulphur-yellow mounds of *Euphorbia palustris*. These are quickly followed by the grassy foliage and tall flowers of *Iris sibirica* in groups of white or blue. Perhaps the most dramatic effect is that produced when the *Crambe cordifolia* erupts into huge airy clouds of tiny white flowers in early summer. If left, the tracery of branching seed heads remains attractive until autumn gales break the seeds away, blowing them round the garden like so much tumbleweed in an American Western. The huge shiny green leaves beneath provide a pleasing contrast to lesser plants near by. *Thalictrum flavum* subsp. *glaucum* adds further height and interest at the rear, its divided blue-grey foliage topped off with powder-puff flowers of lemon yellow. Astrantias, hostas, hemerocallis, violas, nepeta, phlox and many others carry on and fill out the display.

LEFT Flanked by the pastel borders, a broad grass path leads to the Beech Circle and beyond
CENTRE Clematis-clothed pyramids and viola-filled urns provide early summer punctuation
RIGHT An abundance of tumbling flowers on Viticella clematis 'Grandiflora Sanguinea' provide a darker accent to show off the pastel hues of cleome, astrantia, thalictrum and phlox

The pastel borders: glorious mixtures of herbaceous
perennials, annuals and tender perennials in pink,
mauve and white

TOP Spider flower (*Cleome hassleriana*)
BOTTOM Delphiniums and hostas

It is not just herbaceous perennials that provide colour and interest here. Annuals and tender perennials incorporated among them increase the floral 'hit' with great effect and extend the season. Looser, more natural elements from the annuals' palette often include the old-fashioned, sweet-scented *Nicotiana affinis* and some of the taller ageratums. The quick-growing *Cosmos bipinnatus* 'Sonata' infills the higher middle and back border spaces with flowers in white, pink and rose held above feathery foliage. Another large annual grown here is *Cleome hassleriana*. Its large flower heads of pink, mauve and white later develop into whorls of long spiky seed pods, from which it gets its common name of spider flower.

It is fascinating to watch a border like this work its way through its life cycle during the year. As the first shoots are pushing up in early spring, we spread a thick carpeting mulch of spent mushroom compost between them, which provides a rich dark background for the emerging light green leaves. Elements from the yellow and blue spectrum dominate the early season, and in time these give way to pinks, mauves and whites. By late autumn, dark greens have faded to yellows and browns. Then we cut down and clear the plants, tidy the borders and put them to bed for the winter – every few years a bed's turn comes round for digging, composting and splitting – before the days lengthen and the plants shoot forth once more.

The success and impact of these double borders comes from the design principles of reflection and repetition. Plantings on either side of the path mirror one another, and similar groupings are repeated at regular intervals along their length. This area, like so much more at Levens, is effective because the essence of its distinct charm has been distilled. There is a concentration on strong contributing plants. The best are repeated for added emphasis, and the whole is strengthened by being undiluted by an unnecessary show of plantsmanship.

Levens has never relied on expensive hard landscaping, old statuary or even modern sculpture to hold together the elements of its design. Instead it uses the living components of topiary and hedges to give form, grassy areas to provide the equally necessary void, and colour-themed flower borders to give each area a distinctive flavour, rhythm and punctuation.

The massive walls of the beech hedge divide and define the garden

THE BEECH CIRCLE AND HEDGES

The great Beech Circle lies at the very heart of the garden. It is the central hub from which the four main pathways quartering the garden radiate. The massive and ancient hedge from which it is made is fully five metres high and easily as much across; its huge domed archway entrances are taller still. It is a truly impressive structure in terms of size and period presence, with an air of peace within its enclosed space that proves irresistible.

A tour of the garden at Levens Hall in high summer is a floral feast. There is a superabundance of flower colour and scent, foliage texture and form. The eager visitor drinks deeply of this heady draught of visual and sensory treats, then when thoroughly intoxicated, stumbles dizzily into the circle.

Here at last, all is calm. A simple circle of plain green grass backed by dark green vertical walls of beech with a disc of sky above provides rest for tired eyes and minds spinning with images and ideas. This is a breathing space between Levens' set-piece 'big hits', a chance to take stock of what has gone before. It is a welcome opportunity for contemplation away from the visually demanding displays elsewhere. A culinary comparison might be the sorbet between larger, richer, more lavish courses. Like a sorbet, the Beech Circle refreshes the palate, revives an already sated appetite and allows just sufficient pause to ready one for more.

Once your senses have revived, and this restful void has stilled your tingling nerves, there are four exits from which to choose. To the east and west lie the main double herbaceous borders and more full-on horticultural bedazzlement; to the north and south lie shady alleys between tall beech hedges, temptingly offering continuations of that mood of restful contentment.

These walks, closely hemmed in by tall green walls, almost give you the sensation of being within a tunnel of greenery, as the thinning sides of the ancient hedges allow you to see their central structure. The component trees are perhaps 300 years old, and many decrepit individuals have rotten, hollow or propped trunks. During the autumn the glistening white fruiting bodies of porcelain fungus on their old wood shine out eerily from the gloom.

Looking up, in many places you can see the tortured tracery of continually clipped branches twisted into natural grafts fusing each tree to its neighbour. Also visible is a long central slot cut right into the entire length of the hedge top. Here until very recently a plank walkway supported by poles was jammed across the topmost branches. The gardeners balanced precariously on it to clip the central swathe of the hedge top, moving the plank along as they worked, the top being far too wide to reach across from the outside edges. Now gardeners are carried smoothly and safely across to this point within the confines of a hydraulic lift's protective cradle.

Below the trees there is a natural carpet of the native wild garlic (*Allium ursinum*), whose white starry balls of flowers are the highlight of the garden during April. The garlic co-exists in perfect harmony with the beech, completing its annual flowering before the hedge leafs up and casts its deadly, dense dry shade.

As you follow the beech alley south, wings of equally massive hedging open out to left and right, enclosing the Wilderness where this main vista ends at an ornamental alcove in the Ninezergh wall. Going north, the vista's focus is upon the garden gate.

Undoubtedly, the beech hedge is Levens' central stabilizing feature. Its great presence defines the garden's geometry and it is the visual anchor holding and supporting all else.

LEFT Inside the Beech Circle
RIGHT Wild garlic (*Allium ursinum*) carpeting the ground beneath the ancient beech hedge

THE WILDERNESS

The large, broadly rectangular enclosure at the south end of the garden has long been known as the Wilderness. This grassy plot between the beech hedge and garden wall is still home to some ancient limes, the last great remnants of Beaumont's original design here.

When Bishop Nicolson visited the garden at Levens in 1704 and found this particular area worthy of mention in his diary, describing it as the 'maze with Lime-trees, chestnuts, Beech &c', it was unlikely to have been a maze in the way that we understand the term. Nor would it have matched our current understanding of the word wilderness, if by that is meant a wild or empty place. Instead the area would have been laid out to a formal pattern, which included a series of wooded enclosures set between grass paths. The Skyring plan of the 1750s shows radiating walks in one half and parallel walks in the other, with standard trees set within the design. The exact nature of the planting is unclear, but the chestnuts, lime and beech the bishop described might have sheltered a dense understorey of shrubs kept trimmed clear of the intersecting paths.

In time this part of the garden, the furthest from the house, developed a more natural and less restrained atmosphere. However, as the trees grew old, fell or were removed, the space left allowed a brief formal interlude again when it became the setting for two rectangular Italianate pools in the early years of the twentieth century. Latterly it resumed a more natural air. Its post-war incarnation had plant-centred informality reigning here with groupings of Scots pine, Japanese maples and island beds of azaleas.

Now all that has been swept aside to give the space a chance to breathe and live as the extension of the garden that it was always intended to be. Two flanking rows of lime trees cast their dappled shade across open grass. Closely mown paths are incised into the longer rougher background, carving out a new geometry while still carrying echoes of Beaumont's original formal design. This modern treatment of the area has been informed by the past but is not a

slavish recreation. It still works as a designed space within the constraints of current usage and realistic maintenance.

The small triangular building that is squeezed into the far corner of the Wilderness is an original feature that has always been known as the Smoke House. It has been suggested that this is where gentlemen in times gone by went to take a pipe, but in truth, its purpose has been lost in time, and it now serves merely as a shelter from summer storms.

The wall here bordering Ninezergh Lane is in a precarious state in places, having suffered 300 years of Westmorland weather. Its other great enemy has been the proximity of a long row of beech trees planted within a metre of it, the last of which crashed to the ground only very recently. Their massive trunks were just about touching the wall, and as the wind swayed their huge crowns, the root plates lifted, moving the old wall above. The remains of some of the ground-out buttress roots can still be seen at intervals along this stretch.

The stone-built alcove in the wall was erected in the 1920s when the Reynolds family were tenants at Levens Hall. It provides a suitable focus for the main vista through the beech hedges. The intersections of subsidiary axes, linking other pathways, have been marked by the stone plinths placed here in 2001.

This simple area is seen to best advantage early or late in the day as low sunlight strikes across the patterned pathways. Silvery blankets of dew on autumn mornings, or a brilliant dusting of white frost in winter, highlights the sharp edges of this carving by showing them in low relief. Once again it is the interplay of light, shadow and texture that brings life and interest to the scene.

TOP The Wilderness: longer grass, wild flowers and flanking rows of lime trees
BOTTOM LEFT The stone alcove in Ninezergh wall
BOTTOM RIGHT Close-mown pathway patterns define the geometry

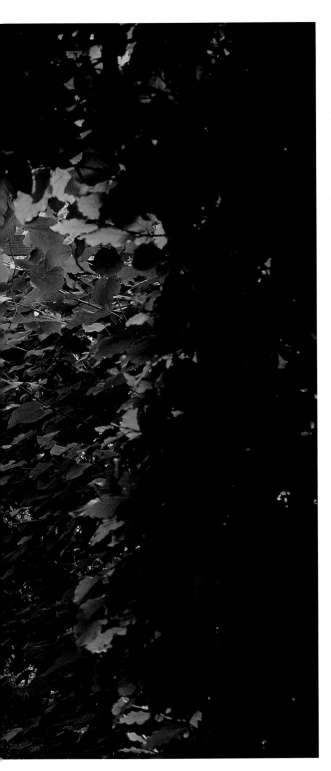

THE FOUNTAIN GARDEN

Road noise could be said to be the garden's prime post-war pest. The enclosing wall may hide the busy A6 from sight, but over it buzzes the near continuous roar of passing cars and lorries. In addition there is the background rumble of fast traffic two fields away on the A590 dual carriageway. Tractors on nearby farmland and mowers or hedge trimmers within the gardens themselves all contribute to an unnaturally noisy environment. When silence does fall, seemingly just for a few moments every year, it is a shocking, eerie experience and awakens us to a realization of the pastoral peace enjoyed by previous generations.

Today's background noise cannot be stopped, but our ears can be distracted from it. This was one of the thoughts behind the new Fountain Garden. The sound of splashing water may not smother other noise completely, but it attracts interest and has a soporific, soothing effect.

Skyring's plan shows that Beaumont quartered this area with a large circle and four cross paths, but further detail is left to the imagination. In subsequent plans it is still shown as a surviving element of the design right through until the early years of the twentieth century, when a hard tennis court takes its place. Post-war necessity saw the whole area ploughed and set to cut-flower production for local sales, before being grassed over in the 1970s as the economics of small-scale market gardening changed.

The renewal of this area was a slow process. First we removed or reduced flanking borders, planted enclosing yew hedges and opened and redefined vistas. We marked out the circle and radiating paths by differential mowing for a number of years to allow familiarization and absorption of the scale of the new feature. It was the tercentenary, in 1994, of the beginning of the garden that gave the necessary impetus to make the dream a reality. The long-awaited formal circular pool was created at last, with a simple single jet fountain at its centre. Four ornamental oak seats created in the estate workshop were placed around it and backed by a circular screen of pleached lime. Linked

The pool and fountain, seen down a pleached lime tunnel

tunnel arbours, again of pleached lime, enclose the entrance paths.

The arbours are made of red-twigged lime *Tilia platyphyllos* 'Rubra', which we pruned back tightly each winter to a roughly espaliered framework. The individual trees have all been trained past each other as an insurance policy against potentially highly visible losses. In spring when the buds at last burst, the soft leafy stems quickly cascade down to produce a wall of fresh green. Summer maintenance is now minimal and consists of merely tying in extension growth and trimming back over-exuberant growth where necessary.

The pool's constantly changing surface reflects sky, weather and the time of day. When still, it is a perfect mirror for the garden's green, the white stonework of the house and the blue sky above. At other times it is in constant movement, its surface ruffled by the lightest wind, by the fountain's white splashes rippling out or by raindrops spattering down under a dull, leaden, grey sky.

Oak benches provide an opportunity for restful contemplation within the enclosing curtains of greenery

The pool is home to a shoal of golden orfe, whose flashes of silver orange often tempt local herons down for a closer look. They leave disappointed, for this pool has been cunningly constructed with deep and vertical heron-proof sides, as the birds need to wade in after their prey from the shallows. The fish have had their share of excitement, though, having made bids for freedom following the floods of 1999, 2004 and 2005. This whole area went under half a metre of dirty river water for a time and the orfe had to be rescued from the ha-ha's ditch as the tide receded.

White water lilies will provide the finishing touch to this area. We planted some when we created the pool, but they declined and ultimately failed. Because of the lack of fresh water entering the system, and the nature of its limestone construction, the water's pH rose too high for their comfort. Fresh rainwater is now piped across from the glasshouse roof, and the stone has been sealed to allow these elegant and fitting additions to thrive.

This is another discrete Levens compartment that satisfies through its essential simplicity. Here there is no unnecessary visual detail to agitate or excite, no buzz of machinery or rumble of traffic to disturb. The sound of the fountain's splashing water dominates, and is consistent and constant. This area has an enclosed, cloistered atmosphere of peace, and it transmits this reflective calming quality to those within it.

TOP Autumn tints calmly reflected in the water
BOTTOM A translucent tracery of twigs

THE RED-PURPLE BORDERS

On leaving behind the leafy stillness of the Beech Circle, you are drawn into the smouldering fiery heat and power of the red borders. These double borders are unified within a colour scheme encompassing reds through to purples and plunging on to deepest blues. The overt intensity of the effect is relieved at intervals by balancing fountains of the silvery foliage of winter-pollarded silver willow *Salix alba* var. *sericea*. *Helichrysum microphyllum*, foaming silvery white along the breaking edge of purple, deepens the contrast further.

Repetition and reflection are again the key to the success of the scheme. The lighter plumes of willow at intervals give height and structure, as do shrubby Rugosa roses 'Roseraie de l'Haÿ'. Their large semi-double flowers of rich crimson purple, like crushed tissue paper,

OPPOSITE Strong contrasts of foliage and flower colour
BELOW Looking back towards the Beech Circle: reds, purples and deep blues dominate the colour scheme

smother the bushes in midsummer, then continue more modestly through till autumn when their large hips complete the display. It is, however, their scent that sets them apart, a powerful, heady and completely intoxicating draught of perfume that floats on the air on warm days.

These are true mixed plantings with shrub, herbaceous and annual contributions. Although by late summer it is the tender additions that make most noise, earlier in the year the more permanent members paint the picture.

Delphiniums and aconitums provide flower spikes of deepest blue, supported within baskets of twiggy hazel. Then, moving through the spectrum towards purple, there is the early low-growing *Stachys macrantha*, its short flower spikes resembling hyacinths. These are followed by bold purple bearded iris and the pincushion red blobs of *Silene asterias*.

PAGES 124–125
CLOCKWISE FROM TOP LEFT
Lobelia with *Amaranthus cruentus* 'Foxtail'; *Dahlia* 'Bishop of Llandaff' and *Canna* 'Roi Humbert'; crocosmia, canna and salix form contrasts beneath the Beech Circle; crocosmia, canna and salix; *Canna indica* 'Purpurea' above lobelia; crocosmia pushing through canna leaves; *Monarda didyma* with *Salix alba* var. *sericea*

Cirsium rivulare
'Atropurpureum' amongst
the silver willow (*Salix
alba* var. *sericea*)

In the middle range, height-wise, is *Cirsium rivulare* 'Atropurpureum', its long-stemmed flowers a very attractive feature of this remarkably well-behaved, non-invasive, non-seeding thistle. Its equally fashionable neighbour *Knautia macedonica* is covered in long-stemmed, deep maroon, scabious-like flowers. *Geranium psilostemon*'s startling magenta flowers strike a note of just sufficient discord to demand notice, while *Astrantia major* var. *rubra*'s starry heads always attract interest. Herbaceous lobelia's brilliant red spikes and sword-leaved fiery-flowered crocosmias complete the foundations of the hardy perennial picture.

The truly outstanding contribution from annuals and tender perennials makes these borders glow from late summer right through to the first frosts. Towards the back are the broad, banana-like leaves of *Canna indica* 'Purpurea' in deepest bronze. They give a warm subtropical effect, but their crowning spikes of exotic flowers veer too closely towards orange for the colour scheme here and so we snap them off early. The huge palmate leaves of the annual castor oil plant *Ricinus communis* 'Carmencita' are a similar shade to that of the canna leaves, and their flowers and particularly their spiky red seed pods are a worthy bonus.

The superb, deeply dissected purple foliage of *Dahlia* 'Bishop of Llandaff' would be sufficient alone to earn it a place here, but couple that with its stunning scarlet flowers and this becomes one of the most vibrant and eyecatching features, drawing the eye forward and along the border. The bushy plumes of *Amaranthus cruentus* 'Foxtail' and the deep purple, almost black leaves of *Perilla laciniata* are also regular components.

As in most of the planting schemes at Levens, we are continually trialling and evaluating new plants here. Old favourites also have to stand the test, and if we find them wanting we use them no more.

The garden is not just a collection of plants for their own sake: however beautiful and fascinating they are as individuals, each has a part to play in the bigger picture. It is the elements that individuals can bring to the broader canvas that are important. The effect created in each unique garden compartment has priority and the plants are subservient to that. The repetition of a smaller number of species, conveying the essence of an idea, can be far more effective than an over-emphasis on plant collecting and diversity for their own sake.

These double borders lead directly to the ha-ha's bastion, where garden merges imperceptibly with landscape. The drop here is large enough to keep sheep and cattle on their own side, and the sunken ditch also serves to drain this low-lying land into the River Kent. The avenue of trees leading the eye across the meadow consists of Beaumont's platoons of trees, made into the full avenue we see today in the nineteenth century. Unfortunately these trees, once designed to frame the spectacular limestone cliffs of White Scar in the distance, have now spread with age, obliterating that view. Though it was known virtually from the beginning that they were planted too closely to fulfil their destiny correctly, like much else at Levens no drastic changes were made and the results, good or bad, remain to this day.

From garden to landscape: the view west from the red-purple borders, across the ha-ha to the field and avenue beyond

ABOVE The vegetable
borders in winter: frozen
ground and bare bean poles
OPPOSITE The vegetable
borders in summer:
asparagus 'hedges' and
bean-smothered wigwams

THE NUTTERY
AND VEGETABLE BORDERS

Over much of its long history the garden at Levens was operated in part on a very functional basis. The production of fruit and vegetables for consumption by the family, their house guests and resident staff would have been of prime importance. A head gardener's skill was measured to a large degree by the standards of this work, and by the regimented intensity of cultivation within the kitchen garden.

The house demanded quantities of fresh vegetables and fruit throughout the year, and this was successfully achieved before the advent of deep freezes by forcing early in the season and storing late. Successional sowings and the use of large numbers of very different varieties extended the potential cropping season.

As demand grew at Levens, so did the head gardener's skill, and resources were provided to match. A walled kitchen garden was created in the nineteenth century, just across the road to the south of the house, separating production facilities from the more ornamental garden around the Hall.

During the 1950s, market gardening came to the fore as a way of partially financing the garden's survival, and the kitchen garden and some areas of the main garden were devoted to cut-flower and vegetable production. Even large commercial greenhouses were filled with tomatoes, all destined for local sale.

By the late 1970s, times had changed once more and this scale of commercial horticulture was no longer viable. The kitchen garden was let, production areas grassed over and the glasshouses removed. The new emphasis was to be on attracting and entertaining the 'house and garden' visiting public.

Today, the vegetable borders in the main garden convey a flavour of what might have been available in the past, and more importantly provide a different emphasis for this area, now a highly ornamental and structured garden 'quarter'.

The all-important repetition and reflection, seen down the narrow grass pathways, are provided by wigwams of runner beans. These also introduce an element of height, and serve to unify and define this area. The Italian pole bean 'Viola de Cornetto', which bears attractive large bunches of deep purple stringless beans, is sown *in situ* at the base of hazel pole supports in late spring, and, provided that rabbits or slugs fail to nibble them off,

the plants soon fly up the supports and flower prolifically.

In the arms radiating from the central circle to east and west are perennial plantings. In one direction, leafy permanent crops of rhubarb grow in the shade of the yew hedge, with waxy grey-leaved seakale near by. In the opposite direction, flanking, filigree feathery hedges of asparagus sprout up through summer, restoring the plant in readiness for the push of tender spears the following spring.

The other arms are usually planted with courgettes, both green and golden, and many different varieties of edible and ornamental gourd. The amazingly prolific courgettes are picked over at least twice a week in season. The gourds are left to ripen until the first frosts threaten, providing a colourful and entertaining display in all imaginable shapes and sizes.

The central grass circle, with the sundial as its focus, is bordered by beds fronted by the deep red leaves of beetroot 'Bull's Blood'. These are strikingly backed by the contrasting

LEFT
TOP Summer fullness: bulging 'hedges' of asparagus backed by the Nuttery
BOTTOM Rhubarb and seakale
RIGHT
TOP Purple-podded pole beans mark the paths from the central grassy circle
BOTTOM LEFT The circular central enclosure of the vegetable garden is flanked by beetroot 'Bull's Blood' and backed by the jagged silver-grey foliage of cardoons
BOTTOM RIGHT Pumpkins, gourds and squashes line the pathways by late summer

jagged silver-grey foliage of cardoons. This relative of the globe artichoke was grown in the past for its leaf stems which, when blanched, could be used like celery. Here it is grown as an annual for its amazing leaf texture, size and colour.

The Nuttery, which lies to the rear of these borders, contains a collection of hazelnuts, cobnuts and filberts. The trees are pruned to provide regularity, uniformity and pattern across these grassed areas. They produce nuts too, but since grey squirrels reached here in the late 1990s, it is they who have taken them early and had the benefit.

This area and the role of vegetable growing has changed much over recent years. The changes reflect an acceptance of the altering demands and priorities within a large garden, and although it still provides a flow of useful, garden-fresh and tasty produce for the house, the area more importantly gives another distinct and beautiful garden scene. It could be said to be a triumph of form over function, aesthetic considerations over mere process.

The patterned regularity of uniformly pruned nut bushes

Repetition and reflection: pyramids covered by tall golden hop (*Humulus lupulus* 'Aureus') surround lower box cones, and the yellow colour theme is further emphasized by variegated nasturtiums spilling out along the paths

THE HERB GARDEN

The area that backed on to Colonel Grahme's new south wing was originally the site of the greenhouses at Levens. This working scene would have tied in appropriately with the functional role of the new building, containing as it did a range of domestic workrooms. By the mid-twentieth century, however, the old greenhouses had been removed, new glasshouses had been located further west behind the potting sheds and all traces of the older structures were gone.

This was the area that was the nursery in the 1960s and later became a plant centre selling a range of containerized shrubs from frame beds. A sales operation here, though perhaps a logical enough evolution from what had gone on before, looked unsightly and was incongruous within the main garden setting. Plant sales were therefore moved nearer those essential but less attractive visitor facilities of car parking, toilets and ticketing.

The natural course of action to take with this area seemed to be to follow the fundamental design principle of the garden. So, in an operation reminiscent of Beaumont quartering the garden with cross paths and the great Beech Circle at the centre, we threw out 'the Good earth' and filled 'the walke with the Rubbish', and, finding the soil we had thrown out of the walks 'Good beyond expectation', used it to create 'a deep soyle' in which to plant. In this way we made a design for a herb garden of four beds quartered by cross paths with a central circle.

The new layout was completed in the mid-1980s, and coincided with an upsurge of interest in herb cultivation and use. It was originally planted with a wide variety of medicinal herbs placed quite informally, and the 'cottage garden' effect this gave was charming. The rampant, invasive nature of some of these native plants soon became apparent, however, as did the need for more form and structure to hold the design together.

In the 1990s we modified the area to reflect these concerns. A selection of culinary herbs ousted the medicinal ones. The repetition of box cones around the path entries and four large wooden pyramidal supports placed around the circle provided structure. That central circle and four cross paths are now defined by borders backed by box hedges and containing the herbal interest; and the quarter spaces behind are occupied by matching block plantings. A young yew hedge is slowly growing up around it all to enclose and help differentiate the special qualities of this compartment from the rest of the garden.

The roses lining the entrance walks are aptly the ancient apothecary's rose, *Rosa gallica* var. *officinalis*. This is also known as the Red Rose of Lancaster, though its masses of fragrant, open, semi-double flowers are more of a light rose crimson to our eyes. It is cut back hard after its single early-summer flowering, and regrows again above lavender or purple sage.

The linking colour theme for the area is in yellow orange, strengthening throughout the year. The golden hops *Humulus lupulus* 'Aureus' fly up their pyramidal supports in early summer, painting them yellow. Then their leafy flower clusters, the well-camouflaged 'hops', tumble down. The central circular bed spills over with the bright variegated foliage of *Tropaeolum majus* Alaska Series topped with horned flowers in yellow, orange and red. Its peppery leaves and flowers make an attractive addition to any salad, but here, and also where it is sown to creep out on to the paths all along their edges, it is used to link and unify the area.

In the rear 'quarters', sunflowers provide a strong visual reinforcement to the golden theme and although sadly fleeting in flower, their seed heads prove very attractive to birds later in the season. We use the low-growing, multi-branched variety *Helianthus annus* 'Pacino', though here as in most places in the garden we often experiment. We sometimes place cardoons in the back quarters, and their huge, silvery-white jagged leaves contrast well with the dark yew hedge behind. We allow them to grow as perennials and in the second year their massive silver stems are topped by spectacularly heavy globe thistle flowers.

LEFT The apothecary's rose (*Rosa gallica* var. *officinalis*) above lavender
RIGHT Early-season foliage contrasts from golden yellow hops (*Humulus lupulus* 'Aureus'), jagged grey cardoons and deep green yew

Though the herbs are now kept subservient to the form and layout of the area, within the reflected and repeated style that proves so effective in the garden as a whole, there is still room for much of interest. There are many varieties of mint including peppermints, spearmints, apple mints and Moroccan mint. Sages, including the coloured-leaved forms 'Purpurea', 'Icterina' and 'Tricolor', are well represented, as are thymes, marjoram and oregano. Chives, fennel and rosemary basically complete this simple but effective picture. Even the planting within the urns fits the theme. The variegated-scented *Pelargonium* 'Lady Plymouth' is the centrepiece, surrounded by the cascading trailing growth of the variegated Swedish ivy *Plectranthus madagascariensis* 'Variegated Mintleaf'.

The hedged enclosure near by was once the tastefully screened site of the compost heaps. It has, however, for a long time now been the 'private garden', a hidden area that the family can enjoy away from the inquisitive eyes of visitors.

ABOVE Variegated *Tropaeolum majus* Alaska Series with dwarf sunflowers and
the huge thistle-like heads of cardoons behind
LEFT Golden sunflower *Helianthus annus* 'Pacino' against the dark yew hedge

URNS AND PLANTERS

The layout of the garden at Levens depends for its effectiveness on being a journey through a series of smaller areas which present very distinctive flavours. The garden is divided up by hedges and screening plantings and its discrete elements are joined together by a rigid grid pattern of pathways. Each compartment is linked to the next through peepholes and archways in hedges, tunnels through growth or other relatively narrow pathway entrances. To lead the eye on and the visitor forward, each vista has its focus, its enticing draw. In many cases these are welcome benches on which to rest and contemplate the scene. Elsewhere there are large old urns that in their late-summer fullness contribute greatly to the scene.

Little is known of the origins of the largest stone urns, which are probably nineteenth-century. The soft stone is hand carved, and although the urns may appear at first glance to be the same, there are minor differences and each is unique. The smaller urns at Levens are, however, identical and of more recent vintage. Based on a crumbling sandstone original, these have been cast in reconstituted stone. Old stone water troughs around the building complete the collection.

In these pots and planters, double daisies, pansies, violas and polyanthus cheerfully announce spring after the long bare months of winter. In their summer form their contents are usually fuller, more extravagant and exuberant.

The line of large urns immediately in front of the Hall are the only ones to have a set summer planting from year to year: the superb trailing *Pelargonium* 'Mrs Kingsbury'. It is studded throughout the season by crimson flower clusters and by early autumn its long lax growth is cascading to the ground. Occasionally it reverts to a lilac pink shade, and we cut out these shoots, to be rooted and grown on elsewhere as a variation on the theme.

Stone urns, shown here with violas and pansies in late spring, frame views and link vistas

LEFT The central feature of the herb garden is an old urn filled with the scented variegated *Pelargonium* 'Lady Plymouth'
CENTRE Stone urns, here filled with dwarf argyranthemums, mark the path on to the Bowling Green.
RIGHT Trailing variegated *Plectranthus madagascariensis* 'Variegated Mintleaf' spills out of the central orchard urn

Fuchsias in various forms are often seen to best effect in urns. The arching branches and slim pendent flowers of *F. magellanica* 'Versicolor' are a case in point. Its vigorous growth and attractively variegated smoky grey foliage make this one of the finest single-species urn plants available. The orange-yellow leaves of *F.* 'Genii' and the white-variegated *F.* 'Sharpitor' with delicate shell-pink flowers also inhabit pots and planters as single species. Elsewhere, the dark purple *F.* 'Thalia' strikes a subtly different note. Its growth is more upright and it carries its long tubular red flowers in close dangling clusters. *F. fulgens* is one of the green-leaved, orange-flowered parents of this group and we grow it where we can indulge its immensely vigorous habit to the full.

Mainstays of the summer bedding display also find their way into these planters. The large and floriferous upright argyranthemums are useful where their bare bases can be hidden by other elements. *A.* 'Butterfly' provides very long-lasting large daisy flowers in yellow, while *A. foeniculaceum* creates a silvery-white feel with its grey foliage and small white daisy flowers.

Begonias of the Inferno Series fill smaller urns effectively. Their fleshy, glossy leaves exude vibrant good health and they are always covered in masses of flowers. *Heliotropium arborescens*

'Chatsworth' supplies wafts of its airborne vanilla or cherry pie scent, while more pungent aromas are provided by the scented geraniums *Pelargonium* 'Lady Plymouth' and *P. tomentosum*.

The trailing component, so essential in most raised planting, is often provided by the variegated Swedish ivy *Plectranthus madagascariensis* 'Variegated Mintleaf', whose long shoots spill right down to the ground by the end of the summer. The felted foliage of the helichrysums in silver grey and yellow is also vigorous and effective in this respect.

Verbenas in various forms add flower colour, but it is the diminutive swan river daisy (*Brachyscome iberidifolia*) that is special. Its loose hanging mats of mossy foliage are covered in masses of tiny bluish flowers throughout the season.

As for maintenance, we mix slow-release fertilizer into the compost at planting time, and thereafter it is just a question of keeping them watered. Early in the season, we can rely on showers to help with this work, but as growth develops, the plants tap the planters' limited moisture reserves more heavily and a good soaking at least twice a week becomes a very necessary part of the maintenance round.

THE PARK

Since Thomas West hailed the park at Levens as 'one of the sweetest spots fancy can imagine' as far back as the eighteenth century, its beauty relative to the increasingly industrialized agricultural landscape outside its walls has only increased.

It covers an area of 68 hectares (170 acres), following the course of the River Kent upstream from the Hall. Flanking enclosures of woodland define its upper slopes and screen it from the farmland beyond. Further fenced and open areas of trees in the rolling grassland add to the part-wooded feel. Steep banking and, in places, low limestone cliffs lead down to the sparkling shingle-strewn river bed.

Beaumont's great oak avenue runs the length of the south side, and many of his 300-year-

The River Kent flows peacefully through Levens Park

old trees stand gnarled and defiant in the face of time. Almost equal in age and character are the platoons or square groupings of trees marching through the landscape, and the column of ancient trees lining the top of the river banking.

From the old waterworn limestone seats throughout the park marking the finest prospects, selected by the family during the nineteenth century, the views are still superb. This is especially so looking west over the river valley towards the setting sun with the dramatic mass of Whitbarrow in the distance.

Recalling medieval times when the park was originally enclosed as a deer park, a herd of black fallow deer still roam here. Numbers have fluctuated greatly over the years; currently there are just over a hundred, with about twenty to thirty being culled annually to maintain that level. They cross the river freely, and the woodland at the north-west end of the park

Beaumont's great oak avenue

is known as the deer sanctuary. It provides a peaceful haven for them well away from disturbance by people.

Black and white Bagot goats roam the land south of the river. These were introduced much later than the deer, in the 1960s. They are a rare breed thought to have been brought back to England at the time of the Crusades, and have been closely associated with the Bagot family ever since. Unfortunately they have already done significant damage to many of the trees, ringbarking even quite mature oaks.

Thanks to the success of the campaign against the dual carriageway that would have passed right through it, proposed in the 1960s, the park can today be enjoyed and appreciated by all. Public footpaths run on either side of the river, and are popular with visitors and locals throughout the year. This is not a public park, however, in the sense of there being unlimited free access, and walkers straying from the footpaths are now just one of the many pressures the park bears as the twenty-first century unfolds.

A shooting syndicate rears thousands of pheasants in the woods for later despatch, and there is a fishing syndicate whose members try their hand at pulling salmon and sea trout from the river. The grazing is let to a local farmer, and wood is harvested from the parcels of commercial forestry flanking the boundaries.

The grey squirrels that have spread to this area from the south in recent years are causing immense damage to the younger trees with their destructive habit of tearing bark off branches in long strips. They will certainly pose a problem to the establishment of plantations in the future.

When ancient specimen trees within the landscape fall or are demolished by winter gales they are replaced. Many have been planted in the rotten centres of the old stumps, so maintaining exactly each tree's position within the design.

The park is rich in bird life and to a certain extent, wild life generally but the grassy sward is noticeably deficient in natural native flora. The combination of years of overgrazing and the insidious creep of modern farming practices have led to this regrettable lack of wildflowers. The area's recent inclusion in a government-funded countryside stewardship scheme should see a reversal of this trend. Lower stocking levels, a ban on fertilizers and pesticides, and the planting of wildflower 'plugs' or plants should in time renew this aspect of the park's beautiful diversity.

Three hundred years since Beaumont laid out the garden and improved the parkland, it is truly remarkable that both have survived and improved through that time. Both part of a single vision, they provide space, form and beauty through the seasons and, I hope, will continue to do so in the years ahead.

OPPOSITE
TOP LEFT A group of black fallow deer crossing the river
TOP RIGHT An old waterworn limestone seat
CENTRE Bagot goats
BOTTOM Ancient trees, and their replacements within the old stumps

ABOVE The gardeners:
Matt, Gary, Chris, Rob
and Ben
OPPOSITE
TOP The modern
glasshouse
CENTRE
The old cedar house
BOTTOM Low polytunnels

BEHIND THE SCENES

The tremendous spectacle that is the garden at Levens Hall, although almost entirely composed of living things, is not of course a naturally occurring scene. It is maintained by a great deal of human intervention and control. It is not exactly a fight with nature, but the work could be described as constraining, regulating and ordering those wilder natural elements in order to organize a bigger picture.

There are currently four gardeners, as well as the head gardener, working full time to maintain and develop the site. We are often ably assisted by willing volunteers. Some of these are school students, perhaps spending time learning new skills as part of their Duke of Edinburgh's award; others are at horticultural colleges and hoping to gain useful experience and a good reference. Some are very active and interested early-retired persons, while others still come for short working holidays from abroad. All are very welcome, and put in as much time as they like when they like. They have made a real difference in recent years, and we very much appreciate their hard work.

Although there are some areas of individual responsibility, the gardeners usually move as a team to do the work in hand. This is a more sociable approach, and we can make an impact far more quickly this way. We also do a lot of work behind the scenes to supply and service the whole.

Perhaps the most intensive areas of operation are the production facilities for the 40,000 annuals and tender perennials used within the gardens each year. A modern 150-square-metre glasshouse, brought into operation in 2000, has proved extremely useful. It has computerized climate control, which means that we can set ventilation, heating and shading parameters to be maintained automatically for differing 'crops' at different times of the year. Heating is by a piped hot-water system, and there is a mist propagation area. By using mobile benching we maximize growing space and reduce that wasted on paths. This is not a pretty Victorian-style greenhouse but a modern, fully functional work unit. Its utilitarian sparseness ensures that it serves its purpose well, but being no display house, it is well screened from public view.

The potting shed is directly opposite, and we spend a great deal of time here in early spring sowing seed, pricking out seedlings, taking cuttings and potting up rooted plants. As the

new glasshouse fills, so plants are hardened off and moved to an unheated, well-ventilated cedar house, and ultimately to the 'frames'. Until recently, traditional brick frames with sloping glass covers filled the frameyard, but now low polythene tunnels have taken their place. We use these more to keep plants dry over the wet, cold Westmorland winter than to shelter them from frost. During the most severely cold weather, however, we give plants here and in the cedar house a covering of fleece.

We grow two main batches of plants for use in the box-edged beds of the parterre. For the spring display, we sow pansies and double daisies in early autumn, prick them out into 'six-packs', and overwinter them in the relatively dry conditions of well-ventilated glass or polytunnels. These are planted out just before the garden opens to visitors at Easter. Early autumn is also the time when we take cuttings of all the tender perennials such as the argyranthemums and heliotropes used in the summer bedding. We root these on a heated bench under mist, then pot them into 'sevens' for overwintering in frost-free conditions. Depending on the size of plant ultimately required, we later either pot them on or use them as stock plants from which we take cuttings in spring.

For the main summer display we sow the seed in early spring, bringing it on quickly in the heated glass. The bedding is grown in seed trays or 7-centimetre-square pots or six-packs. A standardized system using carry trays makes moving plants simpler and allows for them to be given double space (by removing half the plants) as they need more room. All are hardened off, ready for planting out after the last risk of night frost has passed.

The service area caters for the full cycle from birth right round to death and decay. When the plants have

Emptying and cleaning
the glasshouse

served their purpose and are ready for removal or frost has blackened and killed them, we take them to the compost heaps. These are a series of concrete-bottomed, railway-sleeper-lined bays that hold decomposing material from six months to two years. We use them in rotation, and so a supply of fresh crumbly home-made compost is always available. Perennial weeds and woody material not suitable for composting are disposed of in Ninezergh Wood at the bottom of the garden, were they can rot more slowly to become part of the woodland soil in time.

In nature, years do not neatly begin or end on certain dates, and neither are seasons constrained by the calendar; they are a continual round, in which one condition slips imperceptibly into the next. The new year may formally begin on 1 January, though for many gardeners it might be a point in early spring. The gardening year at Levens, however, could be thought of as beginning and ending in late July or early August. Although this is a busy time as we maintain the year's creation, it is also the time to reflect on that achievement and to plan to better it next time around.

The complex management of a large and labour-intensive garden such as this is made easier by breaking up the intertwined processes involved into self-contained operations. This approach to the flow of work also helps to describe it.

In late summer, once the mowing, weeding and edging have been brought up to the mark ,the garden requires less general maintenance than it does earlier in the season. However, if it is hot and sunny, urns and planters, now full to overflowing, need to be watered perhaps every other day. The main glasshouse is emptied and allowed to 'cook', so as to reduce pest and disease carry-over, and the other well-shaded and ventilated cedar greenhouse contains only enough large pot plants to service the house. This is a good time for gardeners' holidays before the real 'new year' work gets begins.

Early autumn is a time for propagation and we cut back general maintenance as work behind the scenes takes precedence. Also the first topiary clipping gets under way on the box shapes, and some of the smaller, newer yew.

By mid-autumn, clipping of the great beech hedge is well under way. The hydraulic lift used to get at its enormously wide top is hired each year. This is one of the largest jobs in the garden and may take two people a couple of months to complete.

By late autumn early frosts have struck, blackening the tender tops of dahlias, cannas, summer bedding and vegetables. We clear these away to the compost heaps, and lift and store tubers. We cut down and tidy the herbaceous borders, filling the compost heaps still higher with the debris. Leaves seemingly fall for months, and we organize a couple of major collections, stacking them over winter before returning them to the garden as an only partially decayed mulching material.

By mid-winter, we have clipped the main topiary, mostly from lightweight scaffold towers, and only the yew hedges are left to do. Pruning the wall shrubs and climbers, pleached limes and nuts is another big winter job. Also at this time we empty out the oldest compost heaps, spread their contents over the parterre beds and dig it in. We spread leaves as a thick mulch along the box-edged wall borders and following frosts and thaw, when they are sufficiently soft, we rake the gravel paths to refresh and renew them.

By late winter, the clipping is at last completed for the year and there should be time for a quick winter project before spring takes off. This is a good opportunity for lifting and resetting areas of border, or laying out new garden features.

ABOVE LEFT Clipping the crowned arch from scaffolding
ABOVE RIGHT Shaving fresh clean outlines with a long-reach hedge trimmer

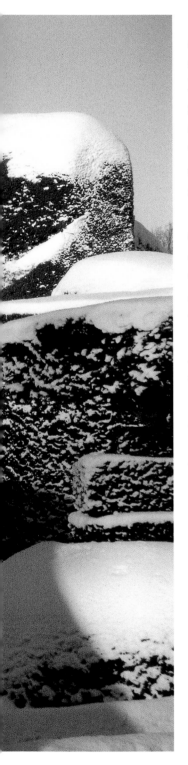

Early spring sees the arrival of lorryloads of spent mushroom compost, which we spread as a thick, weed-suppressing mulch over every herbaceous border. Spring really arrives under glass as we turn up the heat and sow the first of the summer bedding seed and, alongside this, we take cuttings of the tender perennials and pot up stock plants as they come into active growth.

The last few weeks before Easter opening are hectic. We plant out the thousands of overwintered double daisies and pansies in the box-edged beds, mow lawns and cut edges. We put out benches and set signs and safety barriers in place. The pressure is really on behind the scenes too, as thousands of young seedlings need to be pricked out in the short opportunity between their being too tiny to hold and, just days later, too large and drawn to be separated.

OPPOSITE A rare covering of snow
ABOVE Planting out the heliotrope

In the garden, we support fast-growing herbaceous plants with twiggy hazel baskets or stout stakes and string, and, as the last late frosts diminish, move summer bedding plants outside to harden off. We sow runner beans at the bottom of their poles, and plant out sweet peas against theirs. We cut down long grass where spring bulbs were grown, or where it has been allowed for design reasons.

Late spring sees the final big push of the season as we remove all the double daisies and pansies and throw them on the compost heaps, cultivate the soil and plant out the summer bedding to take their place. Once all the bedding is in, we plant the tender annual infilling down the herbaceous borders and at long last we can clear the glasshouses and frameyard of any surplus plants. All lawns are mown once a week, edges cut and weeds hoed or hand pulled in a constant, careful and concerted effort to maintain the highest possible standards throughout the rest of the summer.

THE FUTURE

Throughout the garden's long history, Levens' gardeners have faced the challenges of their day and responded accordingly. Problems continue to arise in many forms, ranging from the day-to-day predations of pests and diseases to the larger, more uncontrollable effects of global warming, pollution and political and economic pressures. All must be met and overcome, and worked around or with.

The topiary, perhaps Levens' greatest landmark, is under threat from a range of diseases. The box edges and shapes are susceptible to various pathogens including the introduced killer box blight *Cylindrocladium buxi*, which has spread across the country. A similar, but less devastating blight, *Volutella buxi*, has been increasing in range and severity in recent years, as has box rust. The plants are old and put under unnatural stress each year when their foliage is cut away. Long-term fungicide spraying would be impractical and totally undesirable, so we hope that renewal of the box edges of the parterre, cultural detailing (by improving drainage and air circulation and reducing shading) and perhaps a long-term change in weather conditions might control the problem.

The yew topiary, too, has its problems. It seems to hold less old foliage in recent years, which gives it more of a semi-transparent, threadbare effect than it had of old. *Sphaerulina taxi* has been diagnosed, another disease that is increasing in its distribution and severity, as is algal growth on the topiary's leaf surfaces in the shadier, damper areas. Once again, spraying these trees and hedges would be impractical and undesirable, so we employ cultural techniques and rely on the plants' own defences, as well as hoping for changing weather patterns.

Perhaps each generation has feared for the topiary's survival, and yet it retains enough in-built reserves and resilience to survive. For this reason, occasional difficulties with pests such as rabbits and hares, slugs and snails, moles and squirrels, sheep and cows, dogs and children all pale into insignificance in the long term. Elsewhere diseases of monoculture such as antirrhinum rust, rose black spot, nicotiana downy mildew, pansy black spot and others may also be devastating at the time, but are likewise just seasonal trials.

We may only be suffering from normal fluctuations in weather patterns, or perhaps we really are seeing the beginnings of long-term change. Levens, lying as it does virtually at sea level, is prone to occasional flooding, particularly when high tides, south-westerly winds and heavy rainfall swell the river. A marker stone measured the extent of the last great inundation in the nineteenth century, but recently – three times now within six years – that level has been far exceeded. Much of the garden, and most of the surrounding fields, were covered as if they were a dirty brown lake. Only Levens Hall itself and the topiary were marginally higher, but less than half a metre more water will see them go under too. There is no conceivable defence

OPPOSITE The garden at Levens is an enriching and educational experience for all ages, and an artistic inspiration to many

against rising sea levels and wetter, windier weather on a global scale. Only time will tell the severity of this potential problem. The results of pollution generally, and global warming in particular, will be for those that follow to record.

A garden such as Levens could, of course, be seen as a very expensive luxury. It certainly was at its inception, in an era very different both socially and politically. Its survival is indeed remarkable, but in order to survive it has adapted. Today, although it is still in private ownership, paying visitors to the garden meet direct expenditure on it, but will this continue to be the case in the future? We can no more guess at gardening fashions to come than we can judge if garden visiting will continue to grow or wane in popularity.

Sustainability is also likely to be a key issue in the garden's future management. High-fuel-consumption tasks such as grass mowing, or the very energy-intensive production of tender bedding, may be questioned and new approaches may be developed. Now that the true cost to the environment of imported composts, fertilizers and chemicals is realized, their use will decline, and the garden will adapt to a new order. The skills, recruitment and retention of staff, and health and safety issues will also be of importance.

Gardening, though, is all about overcoming problems and using opportunities. The fact that the garden at Levens has survived and thrived for so long, not as a static window on a time long gone but as a dynamic and slowly changing scene that is constantly evolving to suit the needs of the day, has ensured that it has a flexibility that well fit it for the times ahead.

Here's to the next 300 years: in the words of the ancient toast given at the Radish Feast, 'Luck to Levens whilst t'Kent flows'.

AFTERWORD

ABOVE The fallen cedar
OPPOSITE Not loss, but
change: the storm has
opened up new horizons

In January 2005, after the text and photographs for this book had been completed, Levens was hit by a severe storm, during which over 150 trees in the garden and park were blown down. The most dramatic impact was in the Topiary Garden, where the cedar of Lebanon crashed to the ground, damaging some of the topiary shapes.

The loss of the cedar that once dominated the scene has changed the view of the house and garden as it had been since the nineteenth century. Out of adversity, however, comes opportunity and, although we are saddened by the cedar's departure, we welcome the possibilities the new space and light will bring.

INDEX

Page numbers in *italics* refer to the captions to the illustrations

AUTHOR'S ACKNOWLEDGMENTS

Generations of gardeners toiled for three centuries and more to set the scene for this book. It is their craftsmanship that is reflected and celebrated in these pages. I am immensely grateful to them all for their pride, passion, skill and determination in bringing the garden to the point at which we see it at present. I must also acknowledge Mr and Mrs Bagot, Levens' owners, for letting me play my small part in that long history. They have allowed me great freedom of expression within the garden, and in granting me open access to the Levens archives they have ensured that its heritage is expressed through my work today.

The seeds of this project were sown by Vivian Russell: it was her prompting of me and persuasion of the publisher that encouraged the idea to germinate. Words alone would not have been enough to convey the visual delights contained within the garden at Levens and I thank her too for her eye for the perfect photograph.

I owe a great debt of gratitude to Julian Munby, who through years of painstaking research has helped make sense of the mountains of historic documents held at Levens in the deed room. I would refer all serious scholars of garden history to his definitive and authoritative work, of which it has been possible to convey only the essence here. I would like to express too my respect for and thanks to Roger Bingham, whose inspirational, educated and entertaining insights into the wider historical and social context have informed my attitude to the past.

I am immensely grateful to Rosemary Webster, through whose encouragement my developing text prospered and strengthened, and whose expert proof readings gave it its formative pruning.

I would like to acknowledge my appreciation, too, to John Nicoll, Jo Christian, Anne Askwith, Becky Clarke and all those at Frances Lincoln who have further transformed this work with their skill, craftsmanship and artistry.

Lastly, but definitely not least, I would like to thank my family: Lydia, Emily and Nicholas. I truly appreciate their support, and sympathize with the frustration they experienced as this book and its subject matter vied with them for my attention. They help shape me, and sustain me, as together we share life in the garden at Levens.

PHOTOGRAPHIC ACKNOWLEDGMENTS

With the exception of those listed below, all the photographs in this book are copyright © Vivian Russell. For permission to reproduce archive material and for supplying the photographs on the following pages, the publishers would like to thank:

By permission of the British Library: 49
Carlisle Library: 51
Chris Crowder: 150
Private Collection: 3 right, 8, 12–13, 14, 16, 17, 18, 20, 21, 23, 25, 26, 29, 30, 32, 36, 41, 42, 46, 47, 48, 50, 52, 53, 54, 55 above, 55 centre, 56, 57, 58, 59, 60 right, 61, 62–3, 64, 65, 67
Royal Horticultural Society, Lindley Library: 55 below, 60 left